FIND YOUR
why
FORWARD

fd
PRESS

FIND YOUR
why
FORWARD

LIVING A LIFE OF
TOTAL CONFIDENCE
& PEACE OF MIND

LINDA FIELDS

FIELD OF DREAMS PRESS™
A *BEST VIEW* IMPRINT
PO BOX 7, MISSION, KANSAS 66201

COVER DESIGN *DFY DESIGN — A DONE-FOR-YOU RESULTS COMPANY*

ADDITIONAL ORDERS AND AUTHOR CONTACT
WWW.LINDAFIELDS.ORG

ISBN: 978-0-9834800-2-0

PRINTED IN THE UNITED STATES

*Dedicated to my husband, Rick,
the man I love.*

Endorsements

"Have you ever wondered why the most successful stars in any professional sport continue to hire personal coaches? They're convinced that to achieve and maintain true success everyone needs continual coaching and an effective support system. Personal and business coach Linda Fields' new book *Find Your Way Forward: Living a Life of Total Confidence and Peace of Mind* is a balanced blend of practical and spiritual instruction--an excellent tool, born out of her life experiences. It's a good read that will serve you very well. Get yours today."

Eddie Smith,
Author and Writing Coach,
International Speaker

"Linda has a wonderful storytelling ability that brings understanding to some of the difficult setbacks that we experience. Her blueprint for moving forward is wrapped in wisdom and simplicity and provides a kick-start to those who have let unrealized dreams go dormant. A terrific and inspirational book."

Deborah Leverett,
Founder, entera+partners,
Leadership Consultant

"Bypassing the traditional western compartmentalized approach that marks our society in our day Linda dares to encompass all the arenas of life in one practical guide within the scope of this book. In this unique practical field guide for individuals who want to make the most of their lives and businesses, Linda addresses personal identity, valuing relationships, business leadership, spiritual direction, and financial blueprints. I have seen many people stop short of living a life of their destiny to know God because they can't make sense of the roadblocks or seemingly delays in pursuing their assignment in life. Not only does *Find Your Why Forward* provide the reader a strategy for overcoming challenges, but it supplies great right-now tools to walk in total confidence in your life and business."

Diane Bickle, Founder
Gladheart Realty

"If you've ever asked, 'Why God?' and not gotten an answer, this book is for you. Don't waste one more day being stuck or stumbling. Linda will show you how to lay down your 'why's' and sprint into your God-given destiny."

Jackie Macgirvin
Author, Angels of Humility

"Linda Fields has a talent for articulating profound concepts with simple, yet powerful words. Her unique style shows through as she uses her own moving life stories to help you unlock your destiny and make a difference in your own life! Don't just read it. This book is a life changing experience!"

Jenn Townsley,
Professional Network Marketer

Acknowledgments

I have many people to thank for their contributions to my life and thus to this work you now hold in your hands. I want to express my heartfelt gratitude to those of you who have supported me, encouraged me and shaped my story by your very lives.

Rick Fields, you are the man I love and now we can go out to long dinners again because I've finished this book.

Heidi and Holly, you are the best consulting agents I know and I will always value conversations with you on any subject.

To my special board of friends and advisors, thank you for blessing this endeavor: Bob and Michele May; Dean and Gina Jones; Lee and Cindy Ullrich; Dave and Peggy Morrison; Herbert and Edith Low; and Scott and Stephanie McKay.

To my Dad who has always known his why forward.

To Ramon Williamson, friend and advisor, with your relentless drive to get to the core message.

To Sybil Thompson, Rhonda Wade, John Ray, Millicent Valek, and CBIT staff for believing in and pursuing opportunities.

Honor is due to John Grable, now deceased, for pioneering a vision.

To sons and daughters who keep us young.

To Bret Mavrich Anne Pedersen, and Christine Scott for help in the trenches to move this project forward.

It is true that no one succeeds alone.

Contents

Introduction

You are probably looking to get more out of life and that is why this book got your attention. You just need a little help, right?

The Problem

Observation indicates that a large percentage of people today are feeling overwhelmed, and facing personal struggles of fear, failure, and disappointment. You may be one of these people, and you for sure know some of these people. They are not sure they can muster up the strength to live full-out any more. What was working yesterday is certainly not working today.

There's been so much change. There's been too much pain. The goal has evolved from thriving in life to just making it. Often, folks look pretty good from the outside. You would not know that they are hopeless, unless you took the time to really look into their eyes and see the despair. People have gotten good at covering up the emptiness aching on the inside, just like actors and actresses playing a part.

Now, I am talking to you. The person you see in the mirror first thing in the morning is the person I am talking to in this book--the same person who occasionally allows himself to recall visions of what might have been before finally able to drift off to sleep at night. You are wondering what it would take to get back into life, full throttle. Is it possible? Do you still have what it takes? Can you still make it?

The Invitation

I invite you to come with me on a journey of wall-jumping, barrier-breaking, heart-wrenching, real-life head-butting episodes in life. After many years, I am opening up my experiences of running into walls so that you will not be surprised when you encounter your own.

As much as we like formulas and systems (and I love them both), we need to see them for what they are. There are an endless number of books on the market that will give you a set of steps, a good story about someone who "made it" to the top of their game, and a charge saying, "You can do this too and be a millionaire in 30 days!" The subtle message is that something must be wrong with you if you don't make it. These books always leave an echo of unanswered questions after you have turned the last page. "But what about the time I tried that and ...? Why did such and such happen? Why did it not work? What did I do wrong?"

The Opportunity to Re-write Your Story

You might have looked at your life as though you are watching a movie and you can't change the ending. But you can. This book is not intended for a casual read. In fact, this book is interactive. I am inviting you into this journey, to engage with me in the process. There will be things I'll ask you to do, to think about, and to write about. This is an authentic invitation for a gut-check from someone who's doing it.

Are you tired of just going through the motions? Do you have a mere inkling that there is more to your life than what you are experiencing now? I dare you to shed all of your excuses and take up the mantle of one who will press through the questions, the confusion, the disappointment, and find their way forward.

I believe your *why* leads to your *way* forward. When you have a nagging "why?" or "why not?," you are faced with a decision to make. It is at this point where you can either move forward to find your way, or stay back at your why. Breaking through this barrier is what I call finding your *why forward*. Your barrier becomes your doorway. This is your big break when you will see hope and expectation beginning to rise over your life like the noonday sun.

About the Walls

In life, you will hit walls. Jesus told us, "In the world, you will have trouble." Consider yourself forewarned. Now, as to your response? Herein lies the real opportunity. Only time and circumstance will determine when you hit a wall, how big the wall is, and how high you have to go to get over it.

But only you will determine how many times you hit the same wall.

Your responses to the challenges you face will determine whether or not you are changed by the walls you hit, the pain they may bring, and the strength of character with which you will emerge.

Some people will tell you that if you are living right, have enough faith, or do things a certain way, you should not expect any trouble. This is a real set up for disappointment. You probably know that by now and are looking for some strategies to help you navigate forward in your life and business.

You may even be thinking you have already blown it, but you are not at the end of your story. You have come to the fork in the road of your responses to life situations time after time. You see two possible paths and one is for greatness. The other is equally accessible, but it leads to despair.

You make decisions every day, small or large, which are shaping your journey and therefore impacting your ultimate destination. It is not too late to steer your course towards a more successful, joyful, and fulfilling life.

The Challenge

The challenge here is getting back INTO the game with an added factor of wisdom. I challenge you to take a good hard look at where you are today, whether you are 20 years old or 70.

Would you like to further develop your potential…

To be the type of person you aspire to become?

To achieve the level of joy and success you desire?

To improve your people skills and grow in leadership?

To learn how to turn obstacles into opportunities?

There are two halves of the battle to stay on course in life.

Strategy and mindset are half the battle. You can be trained and prepared to leap over walls, go around them, or tunnel through them.

The more important half of the battle is the war over the person you are becoming on the inside, the authentic you. From this place flows the ability to execute the strategies in ways that will bring success and move you forward in a sustainable way. When you move forward, you can invite others to come with you. Everyone can see through a façade eventually. Masks don't hold up long term. People know when you are being real.

It is time to get real.

Time to Wake the Sleeping Giant

I imagine that greater joy, the leader within you, and the greatness in your life is like a sleeping giant just waiting to be awakened. It is time to wake the sleeping giant. If not now, it will be harder later (if you ever do it at all).

I will teach you tools and lessons in this book that have helped me. It is my hope that you will be spared some wasted time and energy, have less delay when things get tough, and be equipped in your mind, body, and spirit to pursue your desired destination. I am not promising you that you will have a million dollars in 30 days, nor am I saying you will never have another problem. But I will tell you that if you decide to go on a life quest to the next level, I believe you will have less regret, more joy, and a real sense of peace in your soul. You will become empowered to operate above your circumstances day by day. When you look back on your life later, you will see that you've built a legacy others can stand on. A meaningful legacy is within your reach and I think you should go for it.

If you're still reading, I expect you are throwing your hat in the ring to go on this journey with me. Congratulations on your decision to link arms and move forward. Get ready to step confidently into your greatness.

It's time to wake the sleeping giant.

Believing WITH you,

Linda Fields

Some Instructions:

You are invited to write in this book, to underline or highlight key points. I hope you will wear it out and get one for a friend. I have included extra space for you to jot down what you are thinking and a few blanks to fill in; you can even write in the margin. If that makes you nervous, be sure you get the companion journal specifically designed for you to record your journey. The more you engage with the process the more you will benefit!

A few Texas slang terms made their way into this work; they are duly *noted** and interpreted in the Glossary at the back.

The Bonus Chapter "Pass it On" provides a Discussion Guide for going through the material with a group of friends or associates. DVD lessons and workbooks provide valuable content to guide you through the lessons in *Find Your Why Forward,* available at www.lindafields.org.

Let's get started...

CHAPTER ONE

You Are Not Your Struggle

I am often met with intrigue when I explain to a new friend about my somewhat erratic and often volatile childhood. Then, the intrigue transitions to a blank stare or look of shock as this new friend can't quite reconcile my history with the fact that I became a fairly well-adjusted adult, without any professional counseling save what God Himself taught me. Don't get me wrong: I am all for good, sound counseling when called for. But I am getting ahead of myself.

I was raised by incredible parents. My daddy, Herbert Low, and my mom, Frances Hill Low, came from very humble beginnings. In good times, things were pleasant, loving, and nurturing. For instance, I used to love to ask Mom how she and Daddy fell in love and knew they were to be married. I would perch my chin on folded hands and listen intently as my mother, the master storyteller, brought to vivid recollection her memories of young love. Mom would unfold a story, as only she could, describing how Daddy had been left alone in the world when his mother, father, brother and sister were killed in a car wreck caused by a drunk driver. He lived in an abandoned train boxcar while attending seminary, because he could not afford anything else. He worked as a janitor in the library to pay for school (while studying to be a preacher.) One day in the Southwestern Theological Seminary library, Mom was looking at the bulletin board when Daddy came up behind her and started a conversation with the simple question, "What's new today?" So began the tale of their relationship, dating life, and the big marriage proposal.

Even as a child, I always asked lots of questions. *How did you know? Why? But what if?* As one friend put it, "Linda, you always want to look behind the curtain." I would ask, "But Mom, how did you know Daddy was the one to marry?" She would get a gleam in her eye and give the same reply every time, "Well, Honey, that was easy. The Bible says, 'Every valley shall be exalted, and every hill shall be made low.'" So Frances Hill became Frances Low, and later became my wonderful mother.

On hard days, Mom's emotional struggles became evident as she struggled with depression and would remain in bed in a dark room without strength to face the day. When these times came around, I learned it was better not to bring friends home from school, because I did not know what to expect. But I did wonder at times why I could not have a home where it was safe to have friends over. Even my friends knew something was different in our home. They wondered about it, but graciously made allowances for me, and never put me on the spot. I did not talk about it until years later, and then with only my closest friends. My friends knew that my mom was extraordinary, because occasionally they experienced her ability to make a person feel like they were a special attraction. They loved this about her.

> *You need to know who you are apart from the struggles you encounter.*

Periods of addiction to prescription drugs, bouts with suicidal tendencies, and endless arguments became commonplace. My mom threatened divorce, and my parents discussed who would take me and who would take my little brother. Somehow, though, I always knew when Mom was expressing her real intent, and when it was the meds or the dark illness talking. I never once doubted her love for me, my brother, or Daddy. I knew on some level, even as a child, how to filter out the exceptions to who she really was. I can't really explain that to you, but I can say that I grew up knowing that I was not my mom's struggle.

Nor did I attribute her struggles as shortcomings to her own character. I intuitively knew these things from about the age of seven, and this understanding protected me from emotional scarring that could have made me a different person than who I am today. I did not understand why she had such struggles. I wanted more than anything for her to be free from the agony she fought during these dark times. I loved her more than words can say and would have done anything for her.

I have often said that Mom gave more in her good times than most mothers give in a lifetime. I still believe that. She taught me to pray by my bed at night, expressing the cares of my heart. She would say, "God understands a girl's heart because He made it." I believed her, and found this to be true.

We all know plenty of people who have made a life crusade out of their problems. They have assumed that their struggles equate to their identity. Whether the struggles belong to them or someone else, the transaction to equate struggle with identity is a catastrophic error.

A life is a precious and unique entity meant to be lived, grasped, maintained, fought for, and, at some appointed time, laid down. Each life is unique unto itself. God speaks, leads, and guides the shaping of a life; of course, we can choose whether or not to listen. The pivotal point for me was twofold: first, paying attention to God's voice and second, giving Him room to work in me over and above the struggles. The struggles are sure to present themselves and you may not get answers to all of your questions. Unfortunately, people often allow their identities to become entangled with their struggles. No doubt, your struggles impact your life; but they are not the sum total of your life. You need to know who you are apart from the struggles you encounter. Regardless of the struggles you have encountered, it is time to take 100% responsibility for your life, who you are, and who you want to become.

The lessons I learned about humility from my Dad are still with me today. Here is a man who could have built his life around the things he never had: no family beyond 20 years of age, no money, the son of a poor farmer, no opportunity to be a great success in the world. However, instead of looking inward at his problems, he must have made a decision at some point to focus outward at the opportunities God placed before him.

On occasion, he has told me the story of feeling the call of God on his life to be a preacher when he was in his 20s. He had previously made a decision to be a teacher or an accountant, and was already in college. He was wrestling with God over the decision and could not get any peace about it. He worked in a dormitory and there was a cranky old furnace that made a thunderous noise in the basement. He thought, "Well if I can just get down to the basement where the loud furnace is rumbling, I can get away from this thought. I would not be a good preacher. I am quiet, not flamboyant…"

After spending several hours in the basement, he found even the loud furnace clatter could not drown out the strong impressions from God. He would not let him go. Dad gave in to the idea, and soon after he enrolled in seminary where he met my mother. Afterwards, he began a series of pastorates in small towns, visiting those who were sick, preaching the gospel, and doing the things God had called him to do. My parents were married for 38 years and were faithful to each other. Our family has many joyful stories to tell as well as the accounts of difficult times. Life was a combination of ups and downs and they did their very best. I have tremendous respect for both of my parents.

When my Mom passed away at 63, our lives were greatly impacted. We had suffered a great loss, although we knew she was happier than ever, and finally free from her depression.

After my Mom passed away, and Dad had retired from pastoring, he called me one day to say he was taking a new position. I waited to see what that might be. He was in his 80's by this time.

In the next breath, he said, "Kiddo, I am going to be the Chick-fil-A sample man at the mall." He went on to explain that of all the positions they had open, this is the one where he felt he could be of most help, serving people samples of chicken. I should not have been surprised, but I was. It took me a while to adjust to Dad's new "career."

Over the next 10 years, Dad served over 10,000 pounds of chicken, and was featured in the corporate newsletter as the Super Sampler. Now you may ask what Dad saw in this job. It is quite simple: it was an opportunity to be of service. People noticed how he did his job, how he cleaned the tables, how he put chicken in the mouths of crying children to help out many young mothers.

There is a freedom you step into when you refuse to define your life by your struggle.

When he retired from this position, the community came out, the *'Eat Mor Chikin'* cow was in costume, and Dad once again was serving. But this time, instead of chicken, he was serving his retirement cake. Dad has retired several times, although he never retires from living and helping.

My dad is tall in character and rich in humility, choosing to live his life looking outward at each opportunity to help someone instead of looking inward at his struggles. A conversation with him leaves you knowing that you have talked with a man who knows God and talks with Him often.

Have you become your struggle?

You have your own unique history with its ups and downs. When you look at how you have been raised, and the situations you have encountered, you will undoubtedly think of people who have been a positive example for you. You will also recall certain people who may have caused you to struggle, may not have been nice to you, and may have caused you pain.

I am not encouraging you to drag out all the skeletons in your closet, but I am asking you to look at your unanswered questions, and how they have affected you. Even though you have encountered hard situations in your life, do you need to set yourself apart from your struggle? Oh, we would prefer to have everything in our past all straightened-out and fixed-up. But life is messy, because people are a mess. There is a certain freedom you step into when you refuse to define your life by your struggle.

We need to allow people to have good and bad traits without labeling them either the Hero or the Villain. It is easy to put a person on a pedestal if you consider them a hero. No one stays on a pedestal for long before their humanity shows through and they topple over. Appreciate them for who they are, but cut them some slack for being human.

It is even easier to cast the person who has caused your struggles as the villain.

Truthfully, we are all a mixed bag.

Are you confusing another person's identity with their particular struggle?

How can you value your own life uniquely and live in greater freedom? A good place to start is by restating your identity.

Restate Your Identity

Think of your life and the many attributes and accomplishments that are true about the real you.

What are the characteristics that describe you when you feel most alive?

Most validated?

Most fulfilled?

Take a few minutes and jot them down.

List these expressions of your unique DNA on the left side of your True Identity Chart; List on the right side the circumstances or struggles that you no longer will be allowing to describe your life.

True Identity Chart

How would I describe myself when I am truly being my authentic self?	*What struggle(s) will I no longer allow to define me?*

Write out a statement or proclamation of your life fulfilling your true identity. Today you can begin taking responsibility for your life at a new level.

I am ready to live my life by exhibiting these characteristics and behaviors that reflect my true identity:

I am not afraid. No longer will I associate my identity with past or current struggles such as:

My identity will be reflected in my relationships with others as I am allowing myself freedom to express myself and contribute my best qualities to my relationships. List of my key relationships:

In business or work I'll be bringing my best self to the table. I will be looking for opportunities to contribute more fully and engage productively this week.

An example of how I can bring a solution to a problem or a creative idea might be:

Notes for Action

List three key words that describe your
true identity. Place your note where you
will see it each morning, especially while
you are retraining your mind and your
mouth to live authentically— bringing
out the REAL you.

CHAPTER TWO
Burned But Blessed

As a young teenager, I knew few disappointments in life. The year was 1967 and Daddy, Mom, my little brother, and I had just moved into a country house in South Texas. We were a close family and for all practical purposes, I viewed God as being in His heaven and all as being well with the world. This was a rather simplified view, I now admit, especially since I had already been forced to cope with so much, but that was my perspective nonetheless. It is also a testimony to how God took care of me.

So far my view had worked for me and prevailed unchallenged. However, I stood on the brink of a very rude awakening that would forever alter my life. It is interesting to see how a life can be changed in just a matter of minutes. The tragedy that followed would jolt me into a whole new realm of trauma.

As I dressed for school on a cool February morning, I checked my hair in the bathroom mirror one more time. I had put on a new mini skirt and nylon stockings eager to look my best as any 9th grade girl would. This was the last normal thing I would do for a long time.

In the next instant, a roaring fire ripped through the room with a loud WHOOSH! Flames engulfed my body.

Butane gas had been leaking from the hot water heater, and when Daddy had attempted to light the water heater, the gas exploded, turning the bathroom into a raging inferno.

Working on pure adrenaline, my dad became my savior as he fought the fire and somehow rescued me as well as my brother from the burning room. Screaming sirens, sterile emergency rooms, and white-clad hospital personnel all rolled into a frenetic blur during the next 24 hours as I fought for my very life.

I remember the look on the face of an emergency room nurse as she began to cut off the clothing I'd been wearing so they could assess my burns. I knew by her expression that things were bad. I was slowly becoming aware of the fact that something was really wrong. I remember sinking into shock, not fully able to comprehend what all was going on.

While the emergency nurse and doctors worked on me, a familiar face suddenly peered in the emergency room door: Evelyn Cochran, my Sunday school teacher, had heard about the accident on the local radio station and drove straight to the hospital. Evelyn is a fixture in Wharton, Texas, and she has stepped in to take charge when many people were in trouble over the years in that small community. Now it was my turn. She would prove very instrumental in my life over the next year and remains a significant voice in my life today.

The first night in the hospital I fell into an uneasy sleep. I felt so awkward, with huge bandage wrappings covering both of my legs and my arms. I could not move my legs and could barely move my arms. My lips were crusted from the fire and very swollen. I was so thirsty. Evelyn was the one who sat by my bed and put small pieces of crushed ice to my lips.

During this critical first night, I could feel myself floating up off the bed. This happened several times and each time I would wake up startled thinking I had to try to stay on the bed. I would later find out that the doctors did not know if I would live through the night.

"Would she live? Would she walk? Would she ever have children? What would she look like?" The combination of butane gas, nylon stockings, and flames had made my legs a target for severe third-degree burns. Many questions circulated in our small town as the news of the "Low fire" spread. But the community members did not just talk to one another; they talked to God through the night, asking for Him to help our family, and support came from every direction. Evelyn informed me that Dad and my brother were in rooms down the hall in the same hospital. They had received second-degree burns. My mom had been in another part of the house and, fortunately, was not affected by the fire. She was not doing well at this time and was not able to deal with the accident, because she had other problems she had to face. Evelyn informed me that Mom was going to have to stay with her own mother for a while.

My dad and brother were brought into my hospital room so we could see each other before I would be transferred to a special burn center. Dad was in a wheel chair and my brother, Dan, was on a gurney. We all tried to encourage each other and it was comforting to just see each other's faces. We would not see each other again for weeks. An ambulance transferred me to the Shriners Burn Institute in

Galveston, Texas, for treatment and skin grafts. I had second-degree burns on my arms and stomach, and third-degree burns on my legs. The fire had burned through all three layers of skin on my legs. I remember feeling like I was totally covered by large bandage wrappings to cover my burns.

I felt awkward and full of pain in a foreign bed, as moments turned into days, and then weeks. Over the long weeks I gained strength to eat, and I slowly began to comprehend the magnitude of my injuries. My legs no longer were clothed with nylon hose or even with skin, but instead bore open wounds with the consistency of jelly. I remembered that I had been concerned about the freckles on my legs at one time; now that seemed frivolous. I was sickened by the sight of my legs, not to mention the pain. My life had been spared, but for what? Was I destined to face painful skin grafts as my little hospital roommate had bravely endured? We awoke each morning to hear children screaming in pain.

Each day I endured a very painful process as the nurses changed the bandage dressings on all my burns. The arduous, long process was excruciating because the bandages had stuck to the wounds. There was no way around this grueling daily experience. After the bandages were removed, the nurses would use instruments to peel off any remaining patches of dead skin. It was such a relief when the whole ordeal was finally over; but I was constantly aware it would happen again the next day. I could not bear to imagine what my future would hold.

> *The heat in the kiln rose to seemingly unbearable temperatures, yet the potter knew what the vase could endure as he managed the refining process to bring out a final beauty and luster.*

I had many hours to deliberate unending questions, as I lay confined to my bed, separated from my family, who were each undergoing their own individual recoveries. *Why had this happened to me? What man would ever want me, or be interested in a girl that was burned and scarred? How had things gone so terribly wrong with my life that I somehow deserved to end up in this terrible situation?*

As I asked God these questions, my mind drifted to a story I had heard somewhere in my childhood, of a potter working at his wheel to shape a vessel. The story described a process where the potter lovingly placed the lump of clay on the potter's wheel and set the wheel in motion, while gently forming a unique vessel. The heat in the kiln rose to seemingly unbearable temperatures, yet the potter knew what the vase could endure as he managed the refining process to bring out a final beauty and luster.

At times in the molding process the firm pressure of the potter's hands pressed and shaped the vessel with tender care leaving significant imprints on the clay.

The story goes on to say how ridiculous it would be for the vessel to suddenly sit up and question the potter! And yet that is what I found myself doing in the long agonizing night watches. I asked *"Why? What's going to happen?*

17

Didn't You not see this coming, God? Have I done something wrong? Is this some type of punishment?"

I slowly began to realize that, although I could not fathom why I was in this painful place, I did not really have to understand exactly why, if I really trusted the Potter. I finally got some relief from my mental torment. My questions were not all answered, but I was going to trust the Potter to shape my life in a way that would eventually bring beauty and form beyond what I could imagine. Now this was a hard thing to believe, considering my current situation. What I saw with my eyes was far from beauty: it was chaos, it was ugly, and it would leave me scarred for life. But I was going to be beautiful, because He was forming and shaping my life to reflect Him; I knew this was an invitation into a journey for life.

I had a long way to go and would still have many other questions, but the root issue had been settled for me, even at this young age.

So I gave up the guilt of all the questions. I don't think God minds the questions at all, but I had doubted that He had even showed up for me. Well He did, and I could not see it at the time. But I was beginning to understand He was walking through this with me, though I could not walk just yet.

I concentrated on recovering and focusing on the future, rather than getting immediate answers to my endless questions. I found myself spending days praying for my skin to heal without the dreaded skin grafts. I had a lot of time on my hands and not much contact with people.

The sterile rooms and strict rules allowing few visitors were required because of the high risk of infection on large open wounds. My room had a window to the hallway where visitors would congregate, and the curtain would be closed until visiting hours. One day I could see the silhouettes of two women through the curtain and I began to think this was my mom, whom I had not seen since I was first burned, and my grandmother. I got so excited that they were there. When the nurses pulled back the curtains, it was not them at all. It was two ladies who were there to see another patient. I was so disappointed. I would learn later that my mom had been undergoing a difficult withdrawal from her medications, which is why she was with her mother during my ordeal. This was a turning point for all of us.

I had visits from Evelyn Cochran each week, and others visited me intermittently. One high school friend came to see me and almost passed out (burns are not for the faint of heart). I felt sorry for her, but there was just no way around the bandages, braces, and pieces of dead skin still coming loose. You get a whole new appreciation for skin in a burn center.

After three weeks, my dad and brother were released from the hospital, and Daddy came 'the day they gave him his pants,' as Evelyn put it. He was so precious and so concerned. This was not his fault. but he felt like it was, since he struck the match. But there is no way he would have known about the leak.

In the next days, to my amazement, the doctors recognized something miraculous and cancelled the skin grafts. During routine examinations, one of the doctors said, "We need to watch this, because little patches of skin are beginning to pull together." They did not really know what to think, because third degree burns don't heal without skin grafts from another part of your body or a donor. With all the authority I could muster, as I faced a group of doctors standing around my bed holding their charts, their eyeglasses perched on their noses, I cleared my throat and said... "Well, gentlemen, the Great Physician is on my case." They nodded, obviously musing over the development, exchanging glances with each other, making notes, and went on about their business. There would be no skin grafts. The skin that grew back was delicate, red, and puffy, but it was skin— and I knew exactly Who put it there.

After weeks of rehabilitation, I painstakingly learned to walk again, just as if I were a little child. When I was ready to be released from the burn center, my whole family came to get me, and it was wonderful to be back together in our home. My dad and little brother had healed from their burns, although they still had pain in their ankles. My mom was doing great, cooking meals for the family, and feeling more like herself.

> *I learned to live again with a new hope.*

I had been burned and almost died, but saw my experience as being branded to live with a new hope. My burns would forever remind me that God had seen me through this terrible experience. I learned to live again with a new hope.

Physical therapy in the burn unit brought me into the same room with many other children who had been scarred and maimed by fire. Although the sights were shocking and sometimes nauseating, we had a common bond, in that we had each been burned and we were each being healed. We were learning to live above our affliction. A typical discussion would involve Chris who was getting a new ear, or myself learning to walk, or some other surgery or contraption to help a burn patient move towards functioning normally.

Over the years, the lesson of the Good Samaritan has come to mind repeatedly. The patients in the burn unit were so shocking in appearance that most people on the street would either stare or walk past them without acknowledging them like they would someone 'normal' looking.

(By the way, I have found the word 'normal' to be highly overrated through the years. In fact in our family we used to have a saying about 'getting back to abnormal,' which was more common for us. It helps to have a sense of humor along the way.)

Everyone has been through a fire.

What is your story?

In life, people get burned.

I have found that truly everyone has to face a tragedy, an illness, a major disappointment, a broken heart, a failed business, or an actual fire. Sometimes it is more than one. To tell our stories, and to listen to the stories of others, is to respect our experiences. You can't measure or compare fires. To each individual, his or her fire is a personal encounter with pain. Are you ready to tell your story?

The captivating feature of these stories is the chapter following the fire: *How did you make it? How did you recover? What did you do? How were you changed?*

You see, when you hear my story of how I learned to walk again, you too might believe you can get up from your pain and walk again. When I hear how you have come through your fire, I can take heart that I can learn from your example.

Your Burns, Your Blessings

Take some time here to capture the lessons you have learned, the ones you own because of your personal brush with pain and disappointment.

In relationships, how have you been changed for the better?

In business, what do you know now you did not know before?

What has been your healing story?

Have you looked at the healing stories of others around you?

Will you look past your burns to your blessing?

I found great blessings waiting for me when I accepted my burns, got past all my questions, and allowed God to show me the blessings.

Blessings of healing, peace, learning to reach untouchables, and hoping again were just a few of the blessings unleashed on my life.

Who is the untouchable, the unsightly member, the one who is different, looks different, on the fringe of your society? What makes them so different from you? More importantly, where is your common ground?

Jesus reached out to a leper and touched him. The leper had just told Jesus, "If you are willing, you can cleanse me." In Mark 1: 41 Jesus was moved with compassion, reached out and touched the leper, and said, "I am willing...." I wonder sometimes, are we willing?

Are we willing to risk our reputation and comfort to be inconvenienced? Are we willing to touch an untouchable? Are we willing to associate with someone our society would look down upon?

Who are the untouchables in your life?

Notes for Action

List a blessing that has come from your burns. Be thankful today for the blessings you can see now. Look forward to the blessings yet to be revealed.

CHAPTER THREE

Finding Your *Why* Forward

Young love is a great love in many ways because it knows no fear. It does not know any better than to hope and believe for the perfect ending, and that is not a bad thing. Rick Fields and I met when we were 18, married at 21, then off we went to make a home in a rented trailer. That "tin box" home with the orange linoleum floor was absolutely beautiful to me. I can still see every room in my mind.

I can also remember my terrible cooking. Fried chicken and guacamole, the only two things I could make, looked great on our fine china to me. I did, however, notice that Rick was always hungry. My efforts to fill his stomach provided us with much entertainment and even a few tears over dishes he could not even seem to recognize. We rode to our college classes on Rick's motorcycle, cooked out a lot (we could do hamburgers successfully), and I learned what it was to be in love, and married to someone with a disease that required constant managing.

Rick had been diagnosed with juvenile diabetes at the age of five. He requires daily multiple insulin injections, which have to be adjusted based on what he eats and how much he exercises, in order to maintain an acceptable blood sugar. Although he had been through several bad insulin reactions growing up, by the time I met him, he had learned to manage it well. After all, he had lived with it just about his whole life.

Because he did so well with it, I was not ready for the emergency situation we found ourselves in when he passed out and I had to call the EMT. One evening, he had gone to wash his hands before dinner. I continued making that night's "mystery meal," but then realized he had been gone too long. When I went down the hall to the bathroom and found the big, strong man I had married totally passed out and non-responsive, I panicked. Nothing I did could wake him. I could not even get him to take the honey or sugar his body desperately needed to function. I knew the clock was ticking toward a coma. I called an ambulance.

He had been ill during the week with a virus and we did not realize the toll it had taken on his food absorption, so we had not adjusted his insulin intake. On top of that, we had been motorcycle riding all day in the hills of central Texas. The slow drain of the virus and the physical drain of the ride had caused his blood sugar level to crash. The wicked face of this disease subtly snuck up on us, and now Rick's very life was in danger. Watching Rick lying on a stretcher in the back of an ambulance was a frightening reminder in our youth of his certain mortality. He had been so full of life only an hour before and now was out cold.

A brush with death or trauma makes you grateful for what you have.

26

He was given an IV and his sugar level came back up. We went back to our trailer more thankful than ever to have each other. A brush with death or trauma makes you grateful for what you have. You remember that life is fragile.

When Rick experienced extreme lows, we learned to juice him up with Coke. Constant monitoring became a part of my life, as it had been his for many years. In these early days, we encountered a very special experience. We had been in a deep sleep in the middle of the night when we were suddenly awakened by what sounded like a choral group singing a beautiful high-pitched melody. Once awake, we discovered that Rick was suffering a dangerous drop in his blood sugar level. He was very weak and disoriented.

I got out of bed and gave him the necessary life-giving sugar. As he was downing the sweets and becoming more stabilized, I asked him what had woken him up. I was thinking of the singing. Rick said, "I heard singing, a beautiful singing." As we talked about the sound that had drawn us out of a deep sleep, we could not believe what we were saying. We had both heard it. We were in awe as we each described the same beautiful singing, angelic sounds drifting through the air waking us up to deal with his life threatening reaction. Had we not been awakened at that very moment, Rick's peaceful sleep might have turned into a coma, or even death.

Angel songs? Yes we believe we heard angels singing. Once again, God showed up to help us and brought an angelic choir.

Just as life is full of threats to peace and security, life is full of ways forward. When I look back on the difficulties we have experienced whether it was a physical problem or a stressful business problem in our retail sporting goods store, I find over and over again that we always had a good path forward that became apparent. We were always looking for the best way forward.

Why Me?

We did not know early on that in the next season of our lives we would have two wonderful children who would develop the same life-altering disease. When our children developed diabetes, Holly at 6 years of age and Heidi at 11, the devastating news hit my husband hard because he felt responsible. We asked, *Why God? Why us? Why our children?* These questions were especially painful because we had prayed very specifically many times that this would never happen. We had prayed before our children were born. We had prayed after they were born. We had prayed over our daughters while they slept in their beds as little children. But now the unthinkable had become reality for us.

Again, I never got an answer to why both of our children were afflicted with the disease. In fact, the medical probability of two children contracting the disease from a diabetic father is so low that the doctors were shocked when Heidi was also diagnosed.

After Holly was admitted to the hospital, I distinctly remember being in the elevator just staring at the floor indicator. For a moment, everything seemed to go into slow motion as I thought about what was ahead for us, and for Holly. She had been so brave, but we were all getting rocked with the realization of how life was now very different. So many things to manage, to watch, to guard against, and to juggle were now an every day, every minute responsibility imposed on her life. I felt then that I would always sense a state of emergency over us. I could not see how it would get any easier.

Truly our lives were changed from this point forward. Peace did return with the passing of time and the practice of the things we knew to do. In every instance, there were things we knew to do: the practical steps to move us forward. Did that minimize the pain? No. Did it mean we didn't have to do the hard things? No. Did it change how we got through the pain or handled the hard things? Yes, I believe it did.

My Best Secret

If I were to give you what I would call my Best Secret, it would be found tucked inside the expectation of and watching for a 'way forward.' Oh I could tell you story after story about the trials, but you have enough of your own trials. What you want to know is, *So what? What do you do to move forward when you are in a situation that is so hard you know your life may never be the same again? How do you go on when you can't make sense of your circumstances? How do you find a way forward when you have more questions than answers?*

I believe your *why* can become your way forward. When you have a nagging "why?" or "why not?," you are faced with a decision to make. It is at this very point that you can either move forward to find your way or stay back at your "why."

The breakthrough comes when you make a decision to move past your "why" and find your way. This is a huge decision. This is a major turning point with exponential power to shape your life and sets you up to live out the destiny you have been holding inside for so long. Your destiny is bigger than you are and until you get over yourself and your questions, you're not equipped to take the destiny out beyond yourself. Wrestling with this decision to the place where you say, *I'm not content to stay back at my why any longer. I must go on to build my life, my legacy of joy, leadership, and influence…"* What is it that you hold in your heart that you've got to get out? Coming to terms with the fact that there's more to your destiny than what you have experienced so far, that you have so much more you can give to others by living your life authentically at full throttle unleashes something powerful within you. You will see what was your roadblock before now open up a doorway for you to move ahead. Your why has become your way. You have learned how to *Why Forward.*

> *You will see your roadblock … open up a doorway.*

I believe you have to ask yourself a fundamental question:

What defines your life?

Is it your trial? Or is it your way forward?

Are you more concerned with your problem, or with becoming a solution? Do you find more glory in the negative attention and pity of being in a difficult situation? Or would you like to pave a way forward so that someone else might also be able to join you and travel the same path?

> *Within every obstacle lies an opportunity in disguise.*

Within every obstacle lies an opportunity in disguise. Sadly, many people are not going to choose to get past the big "why question" in their life. That very decision is the obstruction to healing and progress. The "why" has become a point of such pain, bitterness, and resentment that nothing else can grow in that space.

Your Life and Your Business

Life and business are full of great opportunities for love and joy. There is always a battle to be fought when something of great value is available. So what will you do?

What will you expect?

Where will you look?

And how will you speak and walk and travel through life? Moving forward? Or staying stuck? Are you bumping into walls because you are always looking over your shoulder at the past? Will you be content to wonder what might have been?

Love Finds a Way

When you think of where you are in your life right now, what do you see as your obstacles? Although we would all like to ignore the obstacles, you can't move forward until you see what you are up against. A definition of the obstacle will reveal the doorway to advance. So if you say, "*I am not educated*; or, *I missed my chance*; *I messed up in my work*; *I went bankrupt*; *I did not make it in my marriage*; *I've been passed over by love and by life*," my reply to you is, "Good, now we're getting somewhere." You are defining the obstacle, which allows you to size it up and define a path forward.

Your big "why or Why Not" question is either your obstacle or your doorway. Only you can decide which it will be.

Now this is where I am going to get a little pushy with you. What DO you want? Do you really want to get past your obstacle? Or do you find comfort in having a good excuse for not doing anything more significant with your life than you already have? Are you cozied-up with your problem? Has your problem become too comfortable for you to do anything about it? Are you known by your problem? Are you getting lots of pity and attention? Have you woven yourself into a cocoon of familiar trouble?

Do you say things like, "*Oh well, I would do something, but you know I never got to finish school. I would be in ministry, but I was rejected. I would love to do something to help others, but I don't have any funds. I would have been able to be somewhere in life by now, but my friends turned on me, my pastor did not recognize my ability, my boss overlooked me, my husband or wife left me, I got sick, I made a mistake, I took a wrong turn. You just don't know what all I've been through. You have no idea what others have done to me.*"

Let me know when you are done with your excuses. Yes, I said excuses. Excuses come in handy, don't they? When you have an excuse, you don't really have to make anything else of your future. There's not a person on the planet, no matter how charmed their life may seem from the outside, who does not have a nagging personal failure or a recurring pain that rolls around in their head when they try to go to sleep at night.

> *Will you be bold enough to travel the road to build your legacy?*

Is that what you are choosing for a legacy… a missed opportunity? Is that what you want your kids and grandkids and friends to say about you? *"Poor so-and-so. They almost made an impact, but they were too wrapped up in themselves to teach or speak or bless someone. That was a sad life… so wasted. What a shame."*

What kind of glasses are you wearing? Just how are you looking at your situation? What kind of words are you using? How are you talking about your situation? What do you want? The way you view your situation and the way you talk about your situation indicate what is in your heart. What is in your heart makes its way out of your mouth. Some of us need a little cardiac check up and a follow up treatment plan in this area. Get your heart and mind straight and it will affect your vision and your speech.

We need to get two things crystal clear:

1. What favorable impact do you desire to make?

2. What is your obstacle?

Are you man or woman enough to look at your Why and find your way forward? Will you be bold enough to travel the road to build your legacy? A legacy will bless people. A true legacy doesn't hold others back, it advances them and brings them with you.

Sometimes all you have is just hoping and praying that God will show up.

Lots of people think they have to go to a church when they have a problem. You have to know how to work through problems, whether you can get to a church building or not. That is when you realize church is not confined to a building. When I was in the hospital at age 14, there was not a preacher around, not a church I could go to. I did not even have a Bible, and I was too sick to read it even if I had one. So how did that work?

God showed up in answer to my cry for help. That's how.

No fancy words, no sermon or big revival service. It was just me and God in that sterile lonely hospital room.

I love church, but the truth is sometimes the last thing you want to do is go to another service, hear another verse quoted at you, or watch someone smile and pat you on the shoulder when they have no idea what you are really going through.

Sometimes all you have is just hoping and praying that God will show up. Sometimes He does show up just like you thought. Glory!

More often than not, He shows up but you can't quite see Him. He is standing in the shadows while you figured He was a no-show.

Why weren't my girls healed as I had been? Why wasn't Rick healed as I had been? Why did my Mom die from cancer? Why, Why, Why? These questions can drive you crazy, and you don't have anywhere to turn to get away from them.

Where are the answers? Where is God?

But then, if you get still, you can sense that God sees you and your situation. You are not alone.

You have to get still and ask Him to show you where He was, and, if you wait, He will show you. If you don't settle this, you will go on in endless nagging wondering. It fills a mind with doubt and torment. It is to be double minded, and that is a recipe for disaster.

I was teaching this concept at a conference a year ago. I asked the people at the conference to think about a situation when they thought God had not shown up for them. We took a few minutes for people to write and everyone had something on their minds immediately. After a few minutes, I asked them to simply pray asking God to show them where He was during that particular situation.

After a few more minutes, people began to write what was coming to mind. It is not like He doesn't want to reveal these things to us. He wants us to know that He was there. We get hung up when we believe He was a no-show, or He did not do what we wanted Him to do. It is easy at this point to draw a wrong conclusion that says He did not care and did not come through.

A woman in the group had been writing profusely and tears were flowing down her cheeks. Afterward she shared her story.

She had lost a young child years ago and did not think she had been able to grieve appropriately at the time. She loved her child, was devastated as any mother would be, but had not been able to show her grief.

She asked God to show her where He had been in this situation. As she wrote, with tears flowing, God showed her he was protecting the baby in her womb from being affected by her grief because she was pregnant when she lost her young child. A troubling matter that had burdened her for years was put into perspective when she went to God and took time to listen for the answer. She was so relieved as the weight of the world was removed from her shoulders. She was not a bad mother. She had grieved her loss at the time in the way God allowed so as to protect her unborn child. She moved past her "why" to find her way forward.

Notes for Action

Get a new view of your Why becoming
your Way forward today. E.g., Why did
I land in this job? To meet new people
and learn new things I would have
otherwise missed.

Give up the Guilt

When I was 5 years old, my dad, who was the pastor of our church, my little brother, my mom, and a revival team of speakers and singers, were at lunch in the home of one of the prominent families in the church. It was a glorious day: lots of great fried chicken, homemade pies, jokes, and boisterous laughter. Well that is, until I spotted an irresistible temptation in the form of a set of beautiful, golden, squashy, marble-sized bubble bath beads in Mrs. Riley's bathroom. I had never seen anything like them!

I dared to touch the beads as I squeezed them, they seemed fantastic to me—so fantastic that I wanted them desperately! Here is where the trap was set, and I fell into it. I took not just one or two of these mesmerizing beads, but the entire box. I hid them under my beautiful full-skirted Sunday dress, marched out to the car, and hid the package under the seat for a secret retrieval later.

My newly acquired delight came coupled with a huge load of guilt. I had stolen something from a wonderful lady in the church. It haunted me so that I could never enjoy my new delight. Instead, it became a great weight upon my conscience.

My burden of guilt was ever with me until one wonderful Sunday, when I heard my dad talk about how Jesus Christ had taken ALL our sins upon Him, when He died on the cross. I immediately pictured the gleaming golden bath beads in the tidy package – all 12 of them laid out symmetrically in a little box. I secretly wondered if Mrs. Riley had missed them, or had somehow known all along that I was the thief. After all, the little blonde preacher's daughter in the red and white dress had made one too many trips out to the car that day. Maybe the whole church knew! Just when I thought I could not stand it any longer, I took God's offer for all my sin to be taken care of. I felt that my heart would pound out of my chest as I prayed, asking Jesus to forgive me. Finally, I had given up the guilt. The heavy load of this sin, and many others, lifted off of me as if a dam had broken loose. Now peace flooded into my life and I found a life-long Friend, Advisor and Savior!

So what does this story of my childhood have to do with your life? You may find a child's theft of bubble bath beads to be inconsequential. I would argue with you that the big decisions in life are comprised of many small decisions, for right or for wrong. And this one was flat out wrong. I am so thankful I felt guilty, that conviction would not let me rest until I dealt with the issue. Many people are so loaded down with guilt of one seemingly small bad choice after another that they find themselves in a state of moral numbness. The road to despair is cobbled together with stone after stone of guilt. Apathy, inability to make sharp and clear decisions, and the resulting lack of vision come as a result of unresolved guilt.

The road to despair is cobbled together with stone after stone of guilt over wrong decisions.

Unresolved guilt chokes out life. So, the large lesson in the theft of the small bubble bath beads is that you have to unload the guilt.

Think for just a moment if there is something you acquired that brought with it guilt over how you got it?

Have you stolen time from your family to get ahead at work? What you hoped would help your family may be costing you your family relationships.

Have you entered into a friendship with less than sincere intentions? Are you calling it a friendship, but to be honest, you are looking for status through a person you're using as a pawn?

Do you have strained relations with a co-worker or team member because you have, ever so subtly, contributed to gossip about them? Perhaps you have repeated something that should have remained confidential.

Giving up my own guilt has turned into a way of life for me. Now, I give up guilt often, keeping my mind and conscience clear. When I don't, I find myself weighed down, not thinking clearly, and not making good decisions.

Repentance brings refreshing.

You too can "Give up the Guilt"

When you decide to give up the guilt, simply pray to God about the things that weigh on you. Let Him know that you realize you've done wrong things, you sinned, and that you are sorry. Think of it as a transaction: trading your way for His way. Thank Him for what Jesus did for you and believe that He is your own Savior.

You can write out the prayer; sometimes that helps you organize your thoughts.

Some people make prayer a complicated thing, but it is really just conversing with God. There's no special formula or exact words you have to use. Some people never get around to praying because of fear of not doing it right.

You don't want to carry your baggage into the next season of your life.

Opening a dialog with God in the morning, talking with Him throughout the day as you would a good friend, and praying when you go to sleep is a pretty good way to keep the channels of communication open with God.

As you pray about giving up the guilt, think about some specific examples you are concerned about. You will know if you need to follow up in a specific way.

Perhaps you will want to:

- Extend an apology to someone you have wronged.
- Come clean with the family.
- Reach out to co-workers or team members to set right a wrong.

Getting past your guilt will become a way of life. You don't want to carry your baggage into the next season of your life. It is a relief to have a clearinghouse for guilt by way of simple prayer, and follow-up.

When you give up your guilt you have a clearer mind. You are able to sort things out better and make better decisions.

Notes for Action

Ask God to guide you in your decisions today. List any big decisions or projects you have coming up this week.

CHAPTER FOUR

Get a Larger Vision

I rather like the idea of not leaving a great adventure unexplored. "I'd rather have loved and lost than never to have loved at all." This statement was obviously written by a risk taker. When you think about your life vision, you need to figure out how far and how high you want to go. Small thinking is not visionary. You can always stretch further than you realize. Your vision can be larger than it is today, but it needs to be connected to something bigger than you.

Just playing it safe, hanging back, and never taking a risk equals a boring life to me. So, having said that, let me tell you a story of when I was a little girl.

We had a large chest freezer in our house in the utility room right by the door my Dad would come through at the end of a day's work. The freezer had a horizontal surface large enough to climb up on and play. Often when Daddy came home, I would be in that very spot to greet him as soon as he walked through the door. Many times I saw him come in and put his hat down to turn and tease me. My dad is one of those gentlemen made to have a woman on his arm and a hat in his hand, so he is always dressed to the nine's. Even today at 92 he has an array of stylish caps and hats, and he is quite a looker.

> *There's a stretch ... where you can fly or you can fear.*

At this point, the game would start. He would stand close to the freezer and reach out for me to jump into his arms. Squeals of delight came from that room as I took the leap and Dad reached out and caught me. Then, placing me back on the freezer he would up the stakes. Daddy would step back from the freezer a little, and I would jump taking a small risk. The laughter would continue with the thrill mounting as I did it again from a farther distance. Finally, he would stand about three feet from the freezer. I would be wide-eyed with anticipation. Could I jump that far? And could Daddy catch me? The excitement made me laugh and breathe deep. I would bend my knees and crouch down to get the momentum to take the leap as far as I could propel myself. Shrill screams of laughter erupted as Dad reached out with his strong arms and securely caught me. But there was that time in the air between leaving the freezer and making contact with my dad's arms when I felt like I was flying. I dared not look down during that short trip, which seemed like an eternity. As long as I was looking into my dad's smiling face and outstretched arms, I was flying high.

I've named this story my "leap of faith." It represents to me the way God invites us to take risks, or leaps of faith. There's a stretch in there, where you can fly or you can fear. Flying happens when you focus on the smile, the eyes, and those outstretched arms of security from your Father.

Fear happens when you look down at the hard floor. You let yourself think of the circumstances, all the things that could happen or could go wrong. So what would have happened, had my small feet never dared to jump off the freezer? Would I have been safe? Sure thing. Would I have been bored? Sure thing. Would I have known the thrill of jumping and being caught? No, I would have missed it.

So, through life, I've taken several leaps of faith. Here is a more recent one I want to share with you. How much sense would it make for a well-established couple to leave a community where they had invested over 20 years of their lives, raised a family, built relationships, established careers, and enjoyed life? Not much?

That couple, of course, would be my husband and me. Rick and I came to realize that we could make a change and explore new territory or finish out our lives as they were which would have been a fine experience based on what we knew at the time.

So why change? Why leap?

We had loved our lives as they were but began to anticipate what a change could bring as we dared to look beyond our current horizons. Was it wise to make such a change after investing so much of our lives in one place? Little ventured, little gained.

We took the leap. We resigned our careers in the education and training industry, sold our great home, left the church where we had been plugged in for over 20 years, and set out to go to a place and enter a season into which we felt God had invited us. We had several ideas about how this would unfold, and most of them have looked quite different than we expected. There it is again. God shows up, but not exactly like we thought. Now, looking back, there are some things I would have done differently, but we would have 'done it anyway' all things considered.

The emotional effort to transplant two Texans to the snowy Midwest, plug into a new community, and basically start over, required much more of us than we had anticipated. What did we learn?

Trust your heart.

Before you leap, develop a strategy.

Have your inner circle or home team in place.

Don't give people or circumstances too much power in your life.

Don't interpret an uphill trek as a sign that you "missed it."

Always look for the lesson. Always!

Be willing to keep an open mind.

The only way you quit learning is to die.

Would we have missed this opportunity to know life together in a new place, a new way, a new season? Not on your life!

Someone said when you retire you eat out every day and wear pants with elastic in the waistband. Although I prefer to call it re-firing, rather than retiring, we found those things to be true.

But you also learn how to decide what is important.

Three years later, the pants with the elastic waist are gone, the extra pounds are gone, and the light is on in my heart, and I am embracing life with as much enthusiasm and expectation as I ever did. Maybe more.

That is why you have this work in your hands. It is my desire that you will find courage to take risks when you have the opportunity to grow, and to follow God fully to see what will unfold. I am so glad we took this leap of faith.

I have known my husband in seasons of life precious to us both. But we would never have known each other like we do now if we had always chosen the easy route with no risk. No, we are happy to have taken the leap. Did I ask God questions in this season of transition? Oh yeah, I sure did. I always do. I want to know what's going on behind the curtain. But I did not stay there as long this time, back at the *Why?* The *Why not?*

What is your leap of faith?

What have you learned?

Would you trade it for anything else?

The thrill and the security of landing in your Father's arms are worth the jump.

Becoming Part of Something Bigger

What are you a part of that is bigger than you? What cause, initiative, or value are you plugging into that gives you a sense of contributing to a larger vision?

I spearheaded the creation of a corporate training center a few years ago, which gave me a wonderful opportunity to be part of a larger vision. Because it is in my DNA to develop people, the opportunity to create an organization to train people in their professional skills, as well as their personal lives, was a perfect challenge for me. The opportunity to create the center involved many incredible experiences such as:

- building collaborative initiatives
- creating partnerships
- thinking out of the box
- developing high performance teams, and
- impacting lives with training.

My personal vision is to know my God, have strength, and take action to do great exploits giving understanding to many. The opportunity to be part of something bigger, influencing a region with my passion and vision, was a great match.

I have since come to understand the significance of plugging into a larger vision beyond my own work and life and organization. There is a story being unfolded on a global scale even now that filters down to each individual life, with each person having a role to play. When you catch wind of the weight of your story and vision, you gain perspective which functions to launch you much like rocket fuel does for a rocket ship.

For now let's focus on a Region or City Vision and how that affects an Organizational Vision and provides an outlet for you to express your Individual Destiny.

I'll use my own example and work through this hierarchy I have just described.

Global – the whole earth will declare God's glory

Brazoria County, Brazos River – means the arms of God

City – Lake Jackson, Texas – City of Enchantment

Organization – provide learning through training and consulting

Linda – destiny to know God, take action, give understanding to many in the realms of business and education.

So you may wonder what that has to do with your life; how do you fit in to the big picture? Which of these arenas of life are you mainly concerned with?

- family,
- education,
- religion,
- government,
- business,
- arts or
- entertainment?

Great, that's your first clue as to where you fit. You will find yourself working, volunteering, or developing opportunities that utilize your talents and interests in one or two key arenas.

These spheres of society or as some call them mountains of culture simply provide avenues or thoroughfares for your efforts to flow through as you implement what you have to give in society.

Do some research and find the indicators of how your sphere(s) support the vision of your organization or location. Most people have one or two major areas of interest, but you can move between them so don't feel like you have to pick just one. As you scope out the larger meaning, you will become connected to a larger vision which gives added life to your own personal destiny and vision.

Just imagine... what it would look like to see an investment counselor praying with a client who has just watched their retirement fund plummet... then watching the meeting turn into a discussion of strategies to recoup the investment with a newfound faith.

Picture an aspiring artist asking for prayer to begin a production company to bring movies of hope to a hurting world. Can you hear voices of a mother or a father praying with their child for understanding before heading off to school? Think about how comforting it is to a patient to know that his doctor is praying over his surgery. Can you picture a pastor and businesspeople praying together over the city and their businesses with a common vision? Not long ago a governor of Texas prayed for rain to stop a wild fire that was encroaching on Ft. Worth and the rain came. How long will it be before we pray during the good times instead of just the desperate seasons?

When you identify the particular sphere of society you are wired to influence, you will find that you naturally leverage your personal destiny to the specific mission of an organization or geography providing new levels of meaning to your personal plan.

Once we understand that we are part of something MUCH larger than our own little view of the world, our vision takes on the proportions of a rocket ship with the sky as the limit.

- A vision is planted within you.
- A vision is born.
- A vision requires nourishment.
- A vision needs to be clear.
- A vision needs to be trumpeted.
- A vision will be contested.
- A vision requires a strategy.
- A vision is something you carry.

Your vision is not simply another good idea; it is something that you deeply care about.

What is your vision?

When I was a child, I looked into my Dad's eyes when I jumped into his arms. Today I look into God's face when I step into new territory.

Where are you going to look, to fix your eyes, when you take a leap of faith?

The Power of Dreaming Again

Recently I met with a woman, an actress and writer, who had given up on her dreams of selling her own screenplays, which gave expression to important cultural issues she deeply cared about. Through these she had found something bigger than herself and she wanted to plug her skills and talents into the larger picture connected with her vision. But after years of delay and disappointment with no action on her dreams, she had lost hope.

> *"Wow, what power has come from being encouraged to dream again!"*

I had the opportunity to talk with her and bring those desires and dreams to the surface again. This is something I do by profession as well as by my own passion to develop people. As we began the process, she hesitated to respond afraid to voice her dreams again, but said "Oh, you mean we get to dream?!" I urged her on, "Yes, please do!"

With a few planning tools, she put her plans on paper and began to think about them and put some action steps in place. I gave her some tips on meeting with a writing buddy and checked back with her in a few weeks to see how her vision was progressing.

I found a new vitality and courage in her response as she said, "Wow, what power has come from being encouraged to dream again! I thought my dreams were dead, but now I've gotten off my sick bed to sip a cup of broth. At this rate I'll be leaping over buildings soon." She had a book contract underway and a screenplay in negotiation.

"Our deepest fear is not that we are inadequate.
Our deepest fear is that we are powerful beyond measure. It is our light, not our darkness that most frightens us. We ask ourselves, 'Who am I to be brilliant, gorgeous, talented, fabulous?' Actually, who are you not to be? You are a child of God. Your playing small does not serve the world. There is nothing enlightened about shrinking so that other people wont feel insecure around you. We are all meant to shine, as children do. We were born to make manifest the glory of God that is within us. It is not just in some of us; it is in everyone. And as we let our own light shine, we unconsciously give other people permission to do the same. As we are liberated from our own fear, our presence automatically liberates others."

Nelson Mandela

Dare to dream again.

Write a phrase that describes your vision. Describe the bigger picture of your dreams below. What are the dreams and goals that will build out the legacy of your life?

CHAPTER FIVE

No One Succeeds Alone

There are people who know you, and then there are a few people who REALLY know you. And they still love you. These are what I call your inner circle or your home team. They are the ones who will listen and not judge you. These are the people who love you when you are sad, when you are mad, and when you are glad.

When I think of my closest friend, I think of Rick Fields, the man I married a long time ago, and the man I plan to be married to forever. We have laughed about so many crazy things over the years. We cringe to think of some of the stupid things we did when we were young—like sleeping on a picnic table at a roadside park, (we called it camping), until two truck drivers chose the same locale and proceeded to get into a fistfight. Rick got up, looking as big as possible, flexing every muscle he had and some he did not, then loaded our little Pinto station wagon at warp speed and hightailed it to the nearest Holiday Inn. Then, there was the time I got a straw stuck in my nose while we were shopping in a mall—oh yeah, that was a beauty. You will just have to ask me about it. It is too unreal to explain in print.

We have cried with joy over the birth of our two babies. We cried again when they were diagnosed with disease. We have thrilled at sunsets, danced in the garage, and lived a romance that is better now than it was four decades ago. This man is the one I have shared more with than any other person on the earth. He knows me well and loves me still.

A beautiful thing happens when your babies grow up and become friends. The two beautiful women we call daughters are such fabulous friends and partners with us in business, ministry, and life today. I marvel at their wisdom and their creativity. To see them and their great depth of spirit and heart is one of the most incredible experiences of my life. I love their friendships.

Heidi and I had our first negotiation when she was entering the first grade. Her diplomacy kicked in early as she sat me down for a talk. I had just brought home a carload of beautiful clothes for her first grade year. I could just see her in class wearing these elaborate outfits by a new designer that had caught my eye. I had thrown in one practical denim skirt and knit top for what I envisioned to be "casual day" in first grade. Albeit my corporate thoughts and designer approach may have been a bit misplaced for a first grade wardrobe, my intentions were to dress her for success from the get-go. After I laid out all the outfits, I could see her wheels turning. She said, "Mom, I want to talk to you about these clothes. I really appreciate your taking the time to shop and find all these outfits for me to start first grade in, but this outfit, the denim skirt and top is the only one I am going to wear. Did you keep the ticket?"

Now is that a businesswoman in the making at a young age or what? Back to the store we went and this time she accompanied me and made her own choices. One of the things Rick and I realized early on, by God's grace, is that the lives He had entrusted to us were not just little versions of myself or of Rick. They were wonderfully created human beings with thoughts, hearts, personalities, and definitely their own ideas. Over the years I have learned so much from my children. We guided them and presented opportunities for education, life learning, spiritual salvation, and let's just say, they took every opportunity to the fullest, and then some. Today Heidi works in the business world, is an incredible singer (her friends call her Pipes), intentional friend to many, and such a gift to those who get to be around her. She is also hilarious, I might add. She can blow you away with her sharp analytical skills on a business project, move you by singing *Chestnuts Roasting on an Open Fire,* like Natalie Cole, and then crack you up with an impromptu tap dancing routine. She loves to make people laugh. The combination of intellect, love, fun, and depth makes Heidi one of my very best friends. The transition from child to friend over the years has been seamless, because we knew she was a person uniquely created to live her life bringing her own joy into the world.

Holly was born two years after Heidi and surprised us all from day one. We never dreamed of having a redhead or strawberry blonde since Rick has brown hair (well it was brown, now a snowy white) and I am a blonde. But we had a redhead now. Holly was everything you know redheads should be: bold, pushing the limits, and nobody's pushover. Fortitude has served her well, especially when she was called upon to use it as young as six, when she was diagnosed with diabetes. Although she had watched her daddy manage this disease with good success, the news is always devastating when it comes to your own body. And the news came after we watched her melting away before our eyes. The weight loss and a few other symptoms were dreaded signs of diabetes. When the doctor called to give us the bad news, I think we all cried. That's what a family does; you cry together. What we had hoped would never happen had now been announced by the doctor: "Mrs. Fields, Holly has diabetes."

Rick and I both broke down, knowing what was ahead for her in the constant care, monitoring of sugar levels, and shots, shots, and more shots for the rest of her life. Diabetes is a disease you can't always see from the outside, but it is always with you. It affects everything you do for the rest of your life. The burden became a huge, looming, heavy weight that fell over our house. I still remember all four of us piling on the bed and crying together.

> *That is what a family does: you cry together.*

The next day in the hospital, Holly was sorting through her emotions. She looked like Annie, with her red curls framing her little face, and she looked up at me as she tried to make sense of her little life. She was swinging her legs back and forth, a carefree gesture of childhood, while her mind grappled with things that send an adult mind reeling. She asked me a hard question:

"Mom, if I don't take insulin shots, will I die?" I gave her the truth. That's what family and friends do; they tell the truth.

"Yes, Baby, you would. But God has not planned it that way. He has insulin for you to take so you can go on and live your life." The idea of shots for the rest of your life is not a small thing for a person of any age. She thought about it a few minutes more, legs still swinging, and then announced her decision,

"Mom, I think I'll go for it."

What happened in her little yet large mind at that moment was very significant. I had not made this decision for Holly although I would have done anything to shield her from this life burden. Holly made her own decision. Respecting an individual's ability to make a decision based on truth is something Rick and I have valued since our babies were babies. We never wanted to live our lives through our children. It was a wonder to us to have two beautiful people entrusted to us, knowing they would make their own marks in the world. Holly started early by charging a dollar to run blood sugar tests for her little friends using her glucose monitor at school. An entrepreneurial spirit and redheaded boldness emerged from the onset.

Holly has made choices in her life that defy logic, but seem right and good to her. She spends most of her time in prayer for people, churches, and nations to know God. She is a woman of purpose.

Holly's friendship is one you don't take lightly. From early on she has had wisdom beyond her years. I love having discussions about God with Holly and I learn something new every time.

My inner circle beyond these flesh and blood loves of my life enriches me in ways and realms that amaze me when I stop to think about it. Friends have come into my life in

> *That is what family and friends do: they tell the truth.*

different seasons and I would be incomplete without any one of them. They each add dimensionally to me in rich and diverse ways.

Now before I go on to describe the treasures of these friends, I know you must be thinking of dear friends that have crossed your own path. Watch for parallels in your own life as I paint portraits of my inner circle of friends.

Do the Right Thing- Mike:

Mike is my favorite professional friend because in the course of work, we found many synergies to get good things done. Our accomplishments continually drew accolades from peers, who wanted to know, "How did you do it?!" We gave many presentations together showing industry and education wannabe-partners how to put successful training programs in place.

Mike often quoted Peter Drucker: "Efficiency is doing things right; effectiveness is *doing the right things*." He was a great example in the community of going way beyond his job title or responsibility in a large chemical company to chart new territory in industrial education. The education and industry partnership we spearheaded was the crown jewel of the area and visitors from all over the world, including a delegation from Japan, came to see what all the *hubbub** was about.

The friendship that developed was one based on common goals of doing the things that would move people in our community forward in education, safety, productivity, and beyond that equipping people to ultimately succeed in their personal lives.

Mike was not restrained by the lines of normal and I found that invigorating, since I was always chomping at the bit to take things further, higher, and beyond the norm. Mike would end most meetings saying something like, "Linda's the goose with the golden egg."

We were planning a presentation for a professional conference, and laboring over the PowerPoint presentation to convey how a partnership between industry and education had emerged. During the planning session, a light bulb went on when someone used the phrase "marriage of industry and education" and I think we got the same idea at the same time, but wondered "was it too far out?" What IF we put on a wedding and ditched the slide show? Over the next 48 hours, we crafted a wedding where I actually wore a wedding gown with a veil on an academic graduation cap. The groom was an industry leader in a hard hat, and Mike officiated the program as the preacher. The vows reflected responsibilities of education and industry, and drove the point home better than any slide show. As the crowd of 100 professionals entered the room, you could see a few raised eyebrows as they took in the décor. We had the cake, the music, the whole set up. You could see them wondering if they been invited to an industry/education consortium meeting and if they were in the right place. When they were seated, and the music began, we played out an entire wedding ceremony. Even now, when I run into people who attended the program that day, they invariably comment on the presentation they never forgot: the "marriage of education and industry."

I applauded Mike's creativity, and admired his zest to take unprecedented steps to meet needs. Our friendship was based on a common desire to do the unexpected to meet a need. He simply wanted to "do the right thing."

Because our business partnership resulted in great success, it also drew its share of criticism. People do not always appreciate progress when it threatens the status quo. When you move to do great things, you will upset someone's *apple cart.**

Beverly – a real Texas Woman:

Beverly was my professor in college and came to be my mentor for life. When I became a teaching assistant while working on my MBA, I was fortunate to have the office next door to Beverly. This *pistol-packin' mama** was the most dynamic college professor I'd seen up close and personal, and she was real. One time, before going to a professional conference together I spent the night at her house since we were leaving very early in the morning. Her last words before going to bed were, "Now Linda don't get up in the night or I might shoot ya." I did not move the whole night.

To have the privilege of Beverly Chiodo as my friend and mentor is a rich treasure. She motivates her Business Administration university students to recognize positive character traits in those who have meant something special in their lives. Then she has them write letters appreciating these significant people. The endless stories of the relationships restored and the dialogs opened up are real tearjerkers.

Beverly is authentic in her zest for life, love of students, and relentless energy to spark people on. She sleeps with a life size cut out of John Wayne by her bed, a pistol by her pillow, and love in her heart. Now that is a real Texas woman, living life large and not leaving anything on the table. I would love to have just a small portion of her ability encourage sound character and the resulting positive impact on many lives.

Insightful Larry:

Larry should have come to our organization with a handbook of "Larry-isms." I say that because he had his own terminology, a set of endearing expressions, and more importantly, a systematic way of processing thoughts that intrigued me.

Larry was brilliant with several patents to his name. I increasingly valued Larry's keen personal insights over our years of working together. After every client meeting Larry had this incredible ability to decipher what was 'really' going on. He had an uncanny sense of context that enabled him to interpret the nuances of negotiation and forward movement in any effort.

Larry is astute in business, technologically brilliant, and always in the middle of a story. When his laugh rang through the halls, we knew Larry was "in." Larry was a key part of our organization. I highly valued his ability to develop new curriculum. Talking with Larry proved to be an enjoyable excursion whether the topic was volcanoes, the Bible, a scientific principle, or an organizational insight.

> *Friendships are often taken too lightly.*

We have so much to learn from the people that cross our paths. Friendships are often taken too lightly. Larry once advised me not to let my boundless enthusiasm get in the way of pragmatic reality. So I have been appropriately discerned and diagnosed, just what Larry does so well.

Spending time with Larry, I learned to look deep within a person's motives, and I hope I have just a fraction of his laser-like vision.

Dana - Boomerang Friend:

Dana and I connected because I offered to pray for her when I saw that she was teaching a special class and I figured she could use some support. We looked up at some point in time to realize that we had prayed together for over 10 years, raised our children together from kindergarten to high school, cooked more Thanksgiving turkeys than we can remember, and had many long dinner conversations with our husbands and children around the table. I will be forever connected with Dana in a way that has transcended geographical moves now separating us by several states.

Over the years I have heard many people say that they long for a friend. They talk about loneliness and the desire for a friendship that never seems to come along. My first suggestion to them is that they realize they probably are not alone. I recommend that they find a way to give out the very thing they are looking for. When people give, contribute, extend selfless acts of kindness to others, it is amazing how it comes back around. It is just like a boomerang! Giving without expecting anything in return frees them to honestly, authentically invest in the lives of others. The rewards and blessings of such acts are multiplied.

The first time I called Dana on the phone, I offered to support her teaching by praying for her class each week. What developed was a lifelong relationship of praying for each other. I could not count the lists we made on yellow legal pads of things to pray about over the years, much less all the incredible times we prayed, and even better…the many answers to our prayers.

The return to me in this friendship is a great example of what I call the "boomerang effect" of giving. My life has been enriched beyond measure from this friendship, which started with a phone call offering to help.

Sonny – Man Across the Hall:

When I landed in my new job at a community college, the neatest guy (literally) I'd ever seen had the office across the hall. This man was Sonny Miles. I later found out he wrote his dissertation on "Dress for Success" and now I understood why, because he played the part so well.

The integrity and gentle spirit of a strong quiet man is a beautiful thing to behold. I never saw anyone more diligent, more caring and considerate than Sonny Miles. Power did not change him; advancement did not cause him to morph into someone else. A talk with Sonny was always genuine, clear, and productive. But you also left the conversation with a sense that you had been seen and heard and valued as an individual. What a gift. I want to do that.

Patti – Life-Context Friend:

Patti and I became friends in the 9th grade and there was not a thing she could do to stop it! Let me explain why. My family had moved to a new town and I was in a much larger school than I was accustomed to, which literally terrified me. We had moved from a very small town to a medium sized town but to me it might as well have been New York City. The school building spread out over several wings and I noticed right away that there was one girl who was in all my classes: Patti. So I actually followed her around each day from class to class and she did the only noble thing, which was to befriend me. My friendship with Patti would find us going through the rest of high school, college, marriage, and raising children together over the next decades with a family-like love between all of us. In fact we used to say that we had enough family pictures of all of us together that the children would not know which of us were their real parents if anything ever happened and we needed to raise each other's kids. Now that is love!

When Patti's marriage ended in divorce, I felt that I was experiencing some of her pain. One day during this traumatic season, I glanced at a picture of us with our children that had been taken years ago; it was lying on my desk. All of the kids were dressed in their best outfits and were holding their Easter baskets, so young and so impressionable. When my eyes fell on Patti's face in the picture, I began to cry feeling her pain. A marriage that does not make it is hard on everyone: both parties, the children and the friends and family. When you love a friend, you will feel their pain.

> *By my experience you are richer when you get up close and personal...*

The risk of friendship includes pain. It is a given. To love a friend is to be willing to hurt when they hurt, to cry when they cry. Anything less is not really friendship. To wall off your heart, to stay removed from a painful situation, is to refuse to be right up next to a friend in your inner circle. By my experience you are richer when you get up close and personal, laughing together, hurting together— the hallmarks of true friendship.

The other side of this coin is evident when we see people hurting and we realize that we have not gotten close enough to earn the privilege of sharing in their pain. When people refuse to get close or allow someone into that space, they find themselves hurting alone which is a devastating experience and can lead to a lifetime of pain. We were made to live in relationship and we do better together than we do alone.

Because we had built a relationship over the years, I had the privilege of walking with her through the difficult journey of the breakup of her marriage. I count that an honor. Without this friendship, I would have missed out on countless experiences that have enriched my life. Working at a summer camp in the hills of New Mexico together, vacations at hill country motels where the geese chased our children, many cookouts, prayer times, and her infectious laughter that echoes in my mind even now as I think of Patti are just a few examples.

Michele - Divine Appointment Friend:

Michele – now this friendship is like none other I have in that I simply knew I was to be a friend to Michele regardless of whether she reciprocated in the relationship or not. That was a unique position to be in because I don't think she was particularly interested in the relationship at the onset. We couldn't be more different. She's a brunette; I'm a blonde. She likes numbers; I like people. She likes brown: I like bright gold. She's good at Scrabble; I'm good at drinking lattes. She thrives on research; I need to have a meeting. She has a son; I have daughters.

I have had the sad experience early in life of meeting a special gentleman with whom Rick and I both felt we should develop a relationship. I pushed off the nudge and we did not do much about it. His name was Earl and he was in his 60's at the time and Rick and I were in our late 20's. Rick and I had discussed getting to know Earl and how we admired his intellect, wit, and insight and wanted to know him better. Earl became ill and died suddenly. The news of his death shocked us and we were so sorry for his family; we also knew we had missed the opportunity to know and learn from a wonderful man. I promised myself never to ignore such an impression again.

So I paid better attention this time and began the process of reaching out to Michele in what turned out to be a fabulous, roller coaster like friendship.

We became friends at interesting and pivotal times in our lives while we were sorting out major life issues. We would have long talks about theology, relationships, what we wanted out of life, and how to get past our hurts and pains. We were generally trying to make sense of life.

The heavy discussions and the fact that we were both in the middle of raising families, building careers, and navigating through the ups and downs of life made for an intense relationship. We were constantly grappling with large life decisions or issues.

Over the years, so many things had changed in our lives that our friendship took a turn at one point when we did not think it would continue. So we spent a good number of years going our own ways. Over time, the miraculous happened and we were able to build the friendship again into a relationship founded on rich deep truths and life experiences we share to this day. Our friendship history is tried and true.

Most people are not willing to go through the emotional work it takes to repair or mend or even rebuild a friendship when it has tumbled onto the rocks or ended a season. I can say the rewards are more than worth the work it takes to have a "Divine Appointment" friend for life. They are too many to list and too rich to describe adequately. Because of Michele, I have been driven deeper into the intellectual pursuit of theology bearing out what I know in my heart. Since then, we've driven across the country together to conferences, and worked through life's major issues together, and the result is that we have a certain 'knowing' of each other's lives at a far deeper level. I would not have missed this experience with her for anything. It was worth the contending and the re-building.

I was in the car with Michele not so long ago, when she received a call from her doctor with some disturbing news: she had cancer. She was handling it extremely well, but I, on the other hand, had to pull the car over in a parking lot, get out and pace around the car to have a loud talk with God. Yep, I was asking those questions again about a friend I love. So, the journey goes on, the lessons evolve, and the "Divine Appointment" friendship grows.

Peggy - Survivor Friend:

Peggy is the friend who snuck up on me—I did not see her coming and I am so glad I did not miss her. Peg is the most pure, innocent, expecting-good-all-the-time woman I know. I've often said that if I had to be stranded on an island with one other person, I'd pick Peg, because her outlook is so contagiously positive despite any circumstance that might come up. If sharks were swimming around us in the water, she'd be planning a fish fry, and thanking God for our dinner.

Peggy delights in every good thing. With her mouth she speaks only the blessing

> *Become a voice of authentic hope.*

and never the curse. These are traits I will forever cherish in her. Peg learned to sing when she was almost 40. We were riding together in the car one day on a shopping trip and she told me she had always wanted to sing. Then, she did. Those who hear her sing experience such hope and expectation by watching the love on her very face and experiencing the authentic delivery of a message in song.

I've often seen grown people moved to tears touched with Peggy's gift of song while young children decide they want to grow up to be just like her.

Such childlike optimism, faith, and willingness to follow her heart is a blessing to everyone Peggy meets.

The impact of Peg's free spirit on those fortunate enough to encounter her is almost indescribable. You need to *be* that friend and you need to *have* that friend who literally changes the atmosphere with their words. I have notes, cards, songs, CD's, and memories from Peg that will never leave my mind and heart. She is the friend who expects the best in me, who believes in me, and who will see me do the things I was born to do.

Do you have that friend who will be a voice of hope? To whom are you a voice of hope? Contrary to the escape route viewpoint of "some people are just born positive," I want to challenge you to develop the habit; become a voice of authentic hope. Being positive is not pure genetics, but a discipline you should build out in your life. The seed you water is the plant that grows. This begins by realizing the powerful impact of your words. Offer the words you speak as gifts and not jabs. Speak the good things you hope for your friends. The confidence and courage built when you hear someone who knows you speak your dreams out loud to you is an incredibly powerful force.

Gina - The Whole Enchilada Friend:

Well Gina is a friend on every front. Our friendship came in answer to a thought towards God one day when I was driving to a professional conference. I really wanted to meet a friend with whom I could identify on all the different expressions of my life: work, business, corporate training, spiritual matters, social and family arenas. I wanted it all.

I gave a presentation at a corporate training conference and one of the attendees approached me with questions following the presentation. It seemed we hit it off instantly. My new all-around friend Gina and I seemed to have something in common on any subject that came up. We became fast friends and still relish conversations ranging from corporate training and consulting to process flow and organizational development. After talking shop, we can throw our heads back and laugh about something as ridiculous as falling when trying to get in a cab while wearing our new higher-than-ever heels, conversations with our husbands about their conquest of the biggest deer EVER hunted or the largest fish EVER caught, or girl talk with our daughters. We give each other advice on relationship building and then talk to God about it all in the same evening.

Our idea of a good time includes flipcharts, markers, charts, computers, and agendas. We love work, and have learned how to applaud the best qualities we see in each other. Equally important is the understanding that when one of us needs a good talking to, it is on the way! The beauty of a friend with whom you can go through life-threatening illnesses, life changing geographical moves, joys of conquest and trials that could potentially take you out is a joyful palate of friendship to me. Gina is the *Whole Enchilada** with some sauce on top.

Daniel - He's Not Heavy; He's My Brother:

Dan is 4 years younger than I am and I was so excited when he was born. I had even picked out a name from a Bible story for him, Josiah. But my parents overrode my idea and stuck with Daniel. At times in our childhood, I had great responsibility for my little brother due to our Mom's illness, but it was never a burden. I rather enjoyed taking care of him and took the role of Big Sister as an honor. One of our favorite stories is of me at age 7 baptizing Dan who was then 3 repeatedly in the pool after being baptized myself earlier in the week, just passing on what I had learned like a good Sister.

The incredible talent for music in Dan is something I tried to take credit for since I showed him where middle C was on the piano when we were very young, but the truth is he had a natural genius for the piano from the first time his hands graced the keys. He left me behind in musical ability in the first 10 seconds of one brief lesson about middle C.

I admire Dan for his persistence because the life of a musician is no easy road, but he continues on with gig after gig. Every time his hands touch the keys in any venue whether it is a church, a concert hall, or a hotel lobby, his music changes the atmosphere. One of my favorite things to do when returning to Houston is to go where he is playing. I am so proud of my brother. Oh that I would have a measure of his persistence.

God as Friend:

Now that you are thinking that all these fabulous friends have always surrounded me and you are turning green with envy, I will let you in on a little secret. The one who has friends must also know how to be alone.

For a decade, it seemed I could not be found with a friend. My friends moved to other states, got other jobs, got busy, or for whatever reason were absent from my life. *Why was I left to myself in this lonely season?* This was a very good thing and a very painful thing. In this lonely time of isolation, I learned to hear God. I got to know God like I got to know my friends. Lots of long talks

> The one who has friends must also know how to be alone.

with Him on the patio, who knows how much coffee, and pens running dry from filling pages of journals with thoughts, questions, answers, musings, and realizations brought me into a deep reality of remembering who I was, without friends. It is God who formed me in my mama's womb, God who orchestrated the seasons and friends of my life, and it was God who was with me when no one else was around. This experience and time period in my life was a very necessary thing.

Relationship Factors

I have described in great detail some fabulous friends so that you might begin to view your own friendships as unique gifts to value, to appreciate. People are not alike, and frankly, it would be boring if we were.

Some tips on nurturing friendships that have helped me are these:

- Friends must be held loosely and handled with care.
- Friends must be allowed to have other friends.
- We need to cultivate a rich life-giving habit of celebrating friends and their accomplishments.
- We experience pain when our friends hurt.
- Friends shape us and we are not the same without them.
- Friends are investments emotionally, requiring vulnerability, time, energy, and effort.
- Friends can be let go too easily and should be treated as precious.

Who do you consider your Home Team or your Inner Circle?

What qualities do you admire and cherish about them?

How do you contribute to their lives and destiny?

How do you celebrate them?

Decide who the major voices in your life will be. This is something too important to leave to chance.

It is important to line up with people whose character and integrity you admire and whose opinions you value.

In times of great change, especially, be intentional about your relationships. Reach out to galvanize your inner circle.

Reach out to galvanize your inner circle.

Who do you consider a mentor or teacher?

Are you part of a community to run with?

Where do you find your mastermind group of people with whom you can solve problems, create solutions, and brainstorm new ideas?

Retreat to Advance

Plan a weekend getaway with a group of friends to connect with each person's dreams. During this special time, here are things to consider: Look for ways to celebrate what you see in each other. Think of creative ways to call out the best in the individuals in the group. Ask individuals how they will follow-up with each other afterwards. Plan strategies that enable each member to move ahead with their dreams and plans.

Decide:

Who you will invite.

Where you will go.

What you will say to invite your friends to a "Retreat to Advance" weekend.

Notes for Action:

Jot down the names of a few key individuals you need to get in touch with today; begin renewing your relationships.

CHAPTER SIX
Life At Work

I've heard it said that the way a person does anything is the way a person does everything.

Bob needed a change, which is why he approached a Life Coach. He envisioned getting tips and tricks for business, family, and life. But Bob was surprised when, during the first week, the Life Coach asked to accompany Bob on his ski trip. Bob, being a business executive, asked why he, a Life Coach, would want to come on this trip, as he would just be skiing and getting some much needed R & R. The Life Coach brushed off the question and gave him a vague answer. Bob agreed to let him tag along. The Life Coach took the opportunity to observe his client, even videotaping him skiing the slopes. He also took some notes over the course of the weekend.

Later, when Bob asked his coach again why he had wanted to come along on the ski trip, he replied, "Well Bob, if I am going to help you, coach you, I need to know how you work. And the way you work is the way you play. The way you do anything is the way you do everything."

Just like you, the best lessons I've learned in life have come through experience. Experience really is the best teacher despite all the shortcuts we would like to take. Lessons founded on our experiences apply across all realms of our lives. What I learn in my personal life, I can apply in my business, ministry and community life. We are actively building a network of lessons and relationships that interconnect the spheres in our lives.

When I reflect on the different business ventures Rick and I have endeavored, my mind races back to a little sporting goods store we had in the hill country, during our early days of marriage. Rick was hired as manager of the store located just a block or two from the college campus, the hub of activity, energy and sports in beautiful San Marcos, Texas. Everything he learned while earning his business management degree was now a backdrop for real life "Business 101" in the trenches. What we learned in that crazy season was priceless. We hired young college students to work for us, and they became family. In fact, we changed the name of the store to:

We are actively building a network of lessons and relationships that interconnect the spheres in our lives.

The Field House

We worked hard together. Our employees came over after work for cookouts and celebrations. We celebrated engagements and marriages, and sometimes soothed disappointments. They even threw me a 'labor party' to encourage the birth of Heidi, who was overdue. (That was the only time I've ever known her to be late.)

For Rick's birthday one year, our college student employees presented him with a jock-strap with "#1" printed on it, and a card that said something about being his "biggest supporters." The sense of family among our store team provided loads of fun and joy in the midst of hard work.

We built a silkscreen shop in the back of our store and printed the Southwest Texas State University Bobcat t-shirts. Our artist updated the design for the Fighting Bobcat and put Heidi became the highlight of our advertising campaign. (A baby is always good advertising.)

We had a playpen in the store, and family and work blended well together. I would go to the campus to teach Business Communication, come back and change a diaper, then we would draft marketing campaigns and negotiate uniform contracts for the insatiable business of team sports enthusiasts in our college town.

We followed trends from Nike to Puma to Hacky Sacks and enjoyed a 10-year season in the gorgeous Texas hill country, with plenty of college town life beneath a wide-open hill-country sky.

In this priceless learn-as-you-go season of life and work which I dubbed "Business 101" we learned....

- Relationships rule.
- Authenticity is keen.
- Buying and selling is simply finding something of value people want or need, then making the product accessible at a good price.

- Workers are people with hearts and dreams. Workers well-loved will return later to pay for things they stole from you when you were not looking.
- Proofread your ads: In our Trophy and Plaque business, we unfortunately ran a sale on "plagues."
- Watch out for the big boys; especially if WalMart comes to town.
- "Inlets" are needs coming in and "outlets" are solutions going out.
- When we sold our store we learned that we were not our struggle.
- Its season had come, and its season had gone.

And we were the richer for it in more ways than money for having experienced the lessons learned there.

Fast forward to the success of a corporate learning center I put on the ground where 150,000 participants were trained and the primary lessons of success were frankly not from my Business degree or my MBA.

The most valuable skills and lessons in building a successful new venture came from:

1. Business 101 - Learning the practical side of business by buying, selling, providing great customer service, and managing a team of people.

2. Leadership 101 – the SPARK™ system of Leadership, which is a culmination of the leadership lessons I have developed over the years through leading and managing businesses.

3. Wisdom 101 – Lessons from the Bible.
   Some would argue that the Bible is for Sundays or for church and should stay there. But look at what the Bible says in Proverbs 8:1-4 in The Message paraphrase (language we can all understand).

   Do you hear Lady Wisdom calling?
   Can you hear Madame Insight raising her voice?
   She is taken her stand at First and Main,
   At the busiest intersection,
   Right in the city square
   Where the traffic is thickest, she shouts,
   "You—I am talking to all of you, everyone out here on the streets!"

Notice that Lady Wisdom is addressing people in a busy city intersection where business is going on. God is interested in guiding you and helping you with your business: the hiring decisions, the proposals, the negotiations, investors, PR and even the little details. These are things I ask God about in each of our endeavors.

It is really simple to start the day by asking God to bless your business, to show you how to help people, to do good work, and to bless people.

He does hear you…

The way we do anything is the way we do everything.

The way we live at home is the way we run our businesses.

These wisdom ways we know to be true work in every arena of life.

A person will never be more in public than he is in private. Your home life reflects your true values. If you want to know your real values, think about what you do when nobody sees you. To the degree that your authentic character runs through or is evident in the different areas of your life, you are living a congruent life.

What values and ways of doing life are not negotiable to you?

Specifically, how are you bringing these values into the arenas of business, work, and the community?

Notes for Action:

Describe one of your key values. How can you apply life experience lessons at work, business or ministry to carry out this key value?

"Money's not everything, but it is right up there with oxygen."
Rita Davenport

CHAPTER SEVEN
Money

I recently heard Rita Davenport say this about money: "Money's not everything, but it is right up there with oxygen."

You have to have money in our economy to buy and sell, to acquire goods and services, to do just about anything in life, and yet we can get off-track if it becomes too important. Developing a healthy view of finances is a necessary building block for a successful and results-oriented life, business, or ministry.

After managing budgets in the millions, I have a real appreciation for stewarding resources and funding of projects to bring value. There is a fulfillment that comes from using funds well to produce something that fills a need or closes a gap. We are entering into a season of time where I expect to see innovation and creativity blooming. Times of a down economy are often the seedbed for invention and new ideas.

My first job was selling movie tickets at the Rio Theatre in Wharton, Texas. I was 16 years old at the time, and I valued my initial job experience and learned several things about running a business from the owner. I can still remember counting the drawer, stacking the quarters four high, and balancing out the day's activity. It was exciting even then to see that the business had brought in money at the end of a day's work.

Earning a wage is a good and necessary experience providing many life lessons and financial training to learn to manage money and manage your time. In addition to earning a wage you also want to learn to leverage or invest money to see a return. You can work for money, or make your money work for you, or some combination of the two.

Rick and I have always used a team-approach to finances. A unified position on finances and how to manage them well is crucial to any good marriage. Money is also an accurate barometer of what you value. Look at your bank statement to see where you are spending the most money and you will see what you most value.

Money enables you to accomplish your dreams and helps you facilitate the dreams of others. I recommend creating a personal or family life budget that reflects your income, your expenses, and your savings. Beyond that you need a budget for your dreams. By dreams I mean the things you would do if time and money were no object. Often we are so consumed by making and/or spending money that we don't venture beyond ourselves to think about what could be done to accomplish something greater.

Dare to Dream

A good indicator of dreams is looking at what makes you mad. When you see a particular problem or injustice, and your reaction rises up to want to solve the problem, take note; this is

> *Build healthy relationships with the sunlight people and avoid the naysayers.*

one of your hot spots, one of your dream areas. Think of one of these areas for yourself now, something you feel strongly about.

Do you find yourself angered over the plight of orphans? Do you get enraged over stories on the news about battered women? Do you love the idea of creating a boys' home or a homeless shelter?

What is your dream?

Create a *Blue sky** budget to do something about it. What would it take? Buildings? Land? Food? People?

You will be amazed at what begins to happen once you put your dream on paper with a plan to carry it out, because a seed is planted for your dream to be fulfilled. That seed needs to be watered by prayer and by sharing it with someone who may have a similar interest. If you already have your plan on paper, you have added credibility to launch your dream and others will want to come along and help. Watch for these opportunities to share your plan.

We were all created to be part of something bigger than ourselves. Begin planning now. Get ready to walk into that opportunity to do something about your dreams. But don't wait for what you think is the perfect time to get ready. The plan is already planted in your mind and heart; it is a seed. A seed needs to be watered and nourished or it will never have a chance to sprout and grow.

Get ready in advance. Then, you will find yourself ready to talk with others about your dream, and see it begin to grow. Sharing your plan with others who are supportive and interested is like exposing your plant to sunlight. Equally important, you want to guard your plan from naysayers who will dampen your spirits and discourage you. So choose wisely those to whom you will unveil your plan. Look for those who exhibit the same type of attitude and progress you are looking to operate in with your dream; build healthy relationships with the sunlight people and avoid the naysayers.

Creating Value

When you offer a good or a service which creates value, you need to educate people to recognize how it solves their problems or meets their needs; they will want to buy what you have if it helps them and is a good value. It should be a win-win for both parties.

Do you know what the needs are in your field of expertise?

Are you aware of the biggest problems that occur when people work in your field?

Do you know their biggest frustrations?

Recognizing these signals will open doors to be able to explore opportunities and offer solutions, which are more valuable than you may know. Note some signals you recognize now for increased opportunity to meet a need, solve a problem, or present an answer to a question or frustration in your field:

It is Good to Give

An important principle with regard to managing your finances is the principle of giving. Don't wait until you think you have enough money to begin giving; start by giving a portion of what you have now. The Bible teaches us that a tithe is ten percent of what you earn. Prioritize the practice of giving to God and His work. That is a great starting place, and gifts in addition to that allow you to sow into someone else's dream. Helping someone else accomplish a dream is something that comes back around to you as well, another example of the boomerang effect. What you send out comes back.

Review your personal budget and reflect on your spending priorities. You may stumble on a few surprises. So, take note, and revamp your budget and spending to reflect your values and real priorities. Your use of finances should match what you say is important to you.

Begin your "Dream Budget" today.

Pick a charity or a dream of your own where you would like to make an impact. Create a plan and estimate some numbers for your Dream Project. Plan to share it with a friend this week for their input. Plant your seed and water it. Get ready for it to grow.

Outline the key elements of your Dream Project here:

Notes for Action:

Who would you like to bless with a gift this month? Surprise an individual who has a special need, or give to a charity or group that works in the same area of your dreams.

CHAPTER EIGHT
Do It Anyway

Great accomplishments always usher in great criticism. It is probably a good thing I did not know that when the opportunity for success landed on my doorstep in the form of a new job opportunity.

Sometimes what you don't know can be a form of protection.

I had an opportunity to do something totally new in my career that came at just the perfect time for me. I had enjoyed success in the university classroom but yearned for a new challenge. The long faculty meetings found me daydreaming. I did something I've done about every 10 years in my life: ask God for something new. But this time I added a new level to my request. I not only asked for a NEW challenge, but a GREAT BIG opportunity. Before long I found myself in the president's office talking about something new and great and big that the organization wanted to pioneer.

The need had become evident for an entrepreneurial approach to providing training to large corporations by creating a new entity in our organization. While I found the idea of starting something from scratch invigorating, I must admit the size of the challenge was quite overwhelming. The next two years of my life I was inundated with the business of writing proposals, hiring decisions, program creation, designing systems, meetings with people from the heads of companies, and a roller coaster ride of success. The success came in the form of putting flexible corporate training in place to meet a huge demand that created a frenzy of activity. The success of putting solutions in place only led to more opportunity. Our operation was bursting at the seams from the very beginning,

Our clients were happy, our business was booming. Our Team was developing as a high performance team. One of our organization's leaders likened the journey to navigating a white water rafting experience in the wild river of change. We had definitely entered the rapids and the ride was going to get chaotic.

We hired a part time redheaded assistant who had a very small table to work from, and she answered the phone like we were a million-dollar operation. And eventually, we were.

The atmosphere was charged with excitement each and every day. We had exciting contracts coming our way, we had so many obstacles to overcome that it was almost paralyzing at times. You have heard about the "paralysis of analysis?" Well we did not have time to be paralyzed, so we had to punt. The energy and pace of the frantic day made time go by like lightning. I used to enjoy cream and sugar in my coffee, but I can honestly say that by the end of the year I was taking it black with no time to stir in the extras. That is how crazy it was.

The pace was so intense that we had a few blowups (people were always tired and stressed), but we never blew up in front of the customer. I just love that. We'd go behind closed doors and hash out the problem, create a solution, and then head back out front for more. We could not get enough of the heady success of literally meeting and exceeding our customers' needs. It was like a drug; we were on a high.

One day I could see I was going to have to do something to break up the stress, so I thought of an idea that might just work or might make us look like idiots, but something had to give. So I announced on the department intercom that we were going to now have a 'Dance Break'. I played loud music (I think it was YMCA, YMCA...) for 2 minutes and everyone danced. Well it looked like a parade. Everyone dropped what they were doing and began *shakin' and bakin.* * Even the engineers writing curriculum in the back room came out dancing in polyester plaid pants. We laughed, we moved, we breathed, and then we went back to work.

> *Our family still discusses the lessons and stories from those days because they became part of our story.*

I would not have missed those days for anything, as hard as they were. You know most things worth having come at a cost. This season of working around the clock did not last forever, but while it did, my wonderful husband took up the slack at home, and our daughters became interested in the victory or the crash of the day as we all talked each night about our day. One thing that is very lovely to me is that my family allowed me the adventure, supported me in it and celebrated with me along the way. Our family still discusses the lessons and stories from those days because they became part of our story. That's what families do: they become a part of each other's stories.

One client brought a contingency from another state to learn about our partnerships between community, education and industry. Following his visit, he thanked our team for going the extra mile and commented that we were living out day to day what many other organizations just talk about doing. The attention to creativity and focusing on relationships proved repeatedly to be the only way to do business.

Perceptions are reality in the eyes of the beholder. In my eyes we were doing great because our customers were happy and our goals were not only being met, but wildly exceeded. In the eyes of other people in the organization however, the view was not so rosy. People began to attribute layoffs in other departments and their declining business to the success of my operation and I was now the bad guy.

One of the most difficult aspects of this sticky situation is the fact that I had known these people for years and had become friends with many of them and now they were no longer speaking to me. I had become the enemy.

The strained relations, cold shoulders, and criticism were stressful, especially when I was actually fulfilling my commission in the organization. Deciding how to weather this storm of adversity was essential to my sanity. It is so hard to be in a position where there is never really a clearinghouse for the accusations and perceptions to be calibrated to the truth. Of course there are always two sides to every sticky situation (and most times, a third). Being right was no longer the issue, but more importantly how to manage unresolved differences over long periods of time took priority. Being a person who likes clear expectations and closure, this tension weighed on me and I had to learn how to handle it well.

Deciding how to weather this storm of adversity was essential to my sanity.

We all have a desire to be justified when we're under the magnifying glass. I used to dream about marching from office to office of my critics, dressed in my sharp black suit, my heels determinedly clicking down the hall, coffee (black) in hand, and saying something like, "Look, I never meant for our department to take your jobs or your business. This is not against you. We are for you, for the organization. If our division hadn't been created, the organization as a whole would have lost a ton of business." Oh, I had it all planned out. But I never got to deliver those speeches. And I'm glad, because I would only have made matters worse. No one really wanted to hear my thoughts at that point.

People in other departments perceived my success as causing their failure. Layoffs in other departments were perceived as my fault for doing such a great job to meet the needs of clientele and lessening demand for their services. Budgets in other departments got slashed while my revenue was shooting through the roof. Again, it was my fault.

One day I found a picture of me that was in a publication, an article about our burgeoning division, and someone had drawn a face on my picture, and it was left on the table in the break room for anyone who came in to see. Another day the president called me in to talk to me about how I was 'taking over' the space of the other departments, as if I could. I had asked them to share space, but their perception was that I was "taking it."

Success is costly and leadership is lonely. But the lessons are gold. So, take good notes, my friend, when you encounter your own initiation to success. You will need your lessons, and they will help others you are willing to bring along with you.

You will learn to do it anyway, even when you encounter the dark side of success.

> *Yes, success is costly and leadership is lonely.*

Not only did I have to find a way to press through the land mines of change, but also I had an organization to lead through it, and they were all watching me. So I told my department we would be taking the high road and treating everyone really nice and expecting the best of every situation. If your parents taught you to be nice to people, you probably don't know how important of a lesson that really is in life. I mean really nice. I mean genuinely nice, not just putting on airs. People can see through that in a heartbeat. So not only did we have to be nice to people who were talking about us, but we had to like them anyway. So we bent over backwards to set a tone of civility, positive affirmation, and real human affection to others as we passed them in the hall, worked with them on committees, and looked for every opportunity to build a bridge. We were not perfect at it, but we had set a pace, and we were doing our best to walk it out. So we learned to build bridges.

Building a Bridge

Bridge building involves several elements:

1 First there must be a chasm or a space to be crossed over. Well, that was no problem. We had a huge gap between our department and those who felt betrayed by our success.

2 Next, an anchor or pillar of stability to start out from. That was the high performance team we were becoming day by day.

3 Then, material for the actual bridge to be built across the chasm, providing a connection between two entities. Our main material was the environment we created by our decisions to live, talk, and operate above the circumstances. As we took these actions, something of substance materialized beneath our feet. Our actions were creating solutions providing a path for others to walk across on – the bridge was being formed. A bridge takes a very long time to construct.

4 Finally, a landing place, the other pillar or other side of the bridge, which gives access to the desired destination. Interestingly enough, in my experience of building bridges with organizations and people, you have an idea of the landing place, but you can't access it in the beginning stages. You have to start out by faith and walk by faith, even a blind faith.

So in this bridge building process, we determined to take some very specific actions to create a bridge building culture.

Smile and a High Outlook:

Yes, I said smile. We intentionally smiled, greeted others, used their names in a good way, and spoke intentionally each time we had the opportunity to create a connection. The connection could be a verbal greeting, a handshake, a cup of coffee, or a solution to a problem, any problem at all.

Creating an Atmosphere of Expectation:

Professional talk and dress helps to shape an atmosphere. What? Does that still matter? Yes it does. The way a person carries him or herself, the way they dress and speak says something about how they value themselves and what they invite you into with each interaction. Creating something that says, "I value you, and I value what we're working on together" creates a sense of expectation and the hope for something good. It opens the door to creating together. If your expectations are low, it does not much matter what you say in a meeting. It can only go down from there and it does not seem to matter to anyone what happens. You have already decided on a negative outcome.

However when you put a meeting or a conversation or an encounter together with the elements of style and high expectation, then the individuals involved will sense, "Hey they are really looking for a good result, a favorable outcome to this interaction. I better get with it; they are really expecting something to come out of this, something of value." It is a way of inviting people into something they can participate in.

By esteeming highly what you have to offer you give the other person hope of a good outcome. By esteeming what the other individual brings to the table you make a way for a good connection to occur, a hopeful connection that accomplishes a positive result.

Walking Your Talk

During this season I tried many things in learning to build morale.

We had everything at stake and everything to lose. Everyone was watching to see us fail. Everything we did was highly scrutinized by those waiting for us to fall on our faces.

I trained my team during this time that everyone is a leader to someone. Welcome to leadership 101 in the trenches. I had created a system for Leadership and called it SPARK ™ the Leadership Spirit.

*Everyone is a leader...
to someone.*

Leadership is a dynamic quality that can be sparked in others by leaders who are willing to create a spark. Leadership is a lot of work, but it is such an honor. It is a privilege to have the opportunity to speak into lives, build people up, recognize their talent, and aim them forward as a group. We all have some rough edges, and working in a group is a refining process for everyone involved. It requires give and take.

The basic elements of my model are these:

1. Speak Like a Leader

   A leader speaks with high expectations. When a leader opens the door to creativity and innovation in a way that invites people to share their dreams without fear of being shot down, look out! Here come more leaders.

2. Practice New Techniques

   A leader focuses on human relations techniques that reach below the surface of work masks when dealing with other team members. In fact, a true leader goes so far as to cultivate a stimulating environment in an organization that encourages intellectual pursuit while also recognizing the emotional makeup of an individual. Freeing team members to explore with their minds as well as their souls recognizes and engages the whole person. Looking for new techniques and ways to provide a context for emerging leaders to contribute creates a hothouse for creativity.

3. Access Joy and Creativity

   At the age of five, children engage in about 100 creative tasks a day. Sadly, by your mid 40's, this has dwindled to only a couple of creative tasks a day. Think about how often children laugh compared to the number of times most adults laugh in a day. I love to hear an infectious laugh and watch its effect on those who heard it. Everyone instantly wants to know what could be so funny! We could honestly say that a little humor in the workplace is desperately needed. When did you last play a practical joke on a team member and have a little fun? How can you involve more creative tasks in the work day inviting team members to explore their creative genius in systems and processes?

4. Resolve Conflict

You need to know how to facilitate a way for two people to move forward in a healthy way when there is a conflict. Unresolved conflict is stifling and will eventually grow up to bring organizational morale tumbling down. Apply the concept of building a bridge to help two people separated by a problem work through the issues. Pay attention when conflict surfaces in order to open up the communication, give an opportunity to air perceptions, and help to clarify a path forward. This is invaluable to your culture and your progress. Time spent disarming tension is time well spent.

5. Kick it in Gear

Great ideas left jotted down on a notepad or on your computer are just that —great ideas. So this is where you light the fuse. Taking great ideas from mere notes into implementation requires some kick. Sometimes it's a kick in the pants; kick something, and get moving. It is hard to steer a parked car, so you have to get the engine started and go somewhere. You can do a lot with that momentum and then shape and steer as you go.

Good leadership is attractive. It operates like a magnet. Before long I found myself attracting others around me who wanted to do something exciting, something significant. Too often we keep the stakes too low to attract real talent. There's something about raising the bar, issuing a challenge, that is stimulating and invites adventurers to join the team. So for the first two years I worked around the clock. I created new systems on the floor in my living room at night mapping out processes, creating schedules, and writing corporate newsletters.

> Good leadership is attractive. It operates like a magnet.

The bonds of family in our staff created in this season are still in existence today. When you work hard together, play together, and cry together, you are pretty much joined at the hip. A prime example is what happened when one of our team members became very ill. It took a toll on the whole team because she was a leading member and was a big part of our public relations face. We had a department meeting where she told the other team members of her illness. You could have heard a pin drop. It was clear our team had become a family unit.

I had scheduled a staff development day to come aside and cast vision to the group. We had celebrated the milestones we had accomplished together. It was a beautiful sight to see our team of people who cared so much talk about their most meaningful projects. We had applauded each other, truly valued each person's contributions. Next, we were moving into an interactive team building exercise, where the whole group enacted a V formation of flying geese.

We had just read the *Lessons from Geese* and the team was free to act out whatever part they wanted. These lessons were familiar to the team because we had the *Lessons from Geese* framed in our conference room.

Lessons from Geese - Anonymous

Humans, like geese, were created to work together and to support one another. When we encourage each other and support our leaders, we can accomplish amazing things much more than trying to work alone.

Fact 1: As each goose flaps its wings it creates an "uplift" for the birds that follow. By flying in a "V" formation, the whole flock adds 71% greater flying range than if each bird flew alone.

Lesson: People who share a common direction and sense of community can get where they are going more quickly and more easily because they are traveling on the thrust of one another.

Fact 2: When a goose falls out of formation, it suddenly feels the drag and resistance of flying alone. It quickly moves back into formation to take advantage of the lifting power of the bird immediately in front of it.

Lesson: If we have as much sense as a goose, we stay in formation with those headed where we want to go. We are willing to accept their help and give our help to others.

Fact 3: When the lead goose tires, it rotates back into the formation and another goose flies to the point position.

Lesson: It pays to take turns doing the hard tasks and sharing leadership. As with geese, people are interdependent on each other's skills, capabilities, and unique arrangements of gifts, talents or resources.

Fact 4: The geese flying in formation honk to encourage those up front to keep up their speed.

Lesson: We need to make sure "honking" is encouraging. In groups where there is encouragement the production is much greater. The power of encouragement (to stand by one's heart or core values and encourage the heart and core of others) is the quality of honking we seek.

Fact 5: When a goose gets sick, wounded, or shot down, two geese drop out of formation and follow it down to help and protect it. They stay with it until it dies or is able to fly again. Then, they launch out with another formation or catch up with the flock.

Lesson: If we have as much sense as geese, we will stand by each other in difficult times as well as when we are strong.

In light of the illness of our team member, it was no surprise which lesson the group chose for the role play. Everyone chose the same thing, Lesson 5, illustrating what happens when one goose is sick. This goose flies to the back and another takes its place until the sick goose is able to recover and return to position. The team acted this out and flowed in unison as our friend who was ill went to the back and others flanked her side moving perfectly in step with her.

> *Things were in motion and going nowhere but forward.*

The effect was very poignant and a highly charged emotional experience for all of us.

It was common practice to see the team helping each other in general, giving each other rides, helping with meals when someone was sick, making a basket of personalized gifts for anyone who had a special situation. "The show must go on" was the unwritten motto, and the cast of characters played it out until we looked back over a decade later to see a gleaming building in place with state of the art technology, called a "cathedral of learning" by our architect, and echoes of the voices of 150,000 participants who had come to experience the solutions put in place by a team of people who cared.

We had become engulfed in what we were doing and the culture we had established for excellence and leadership. Things were in motion and going nowhere but forward. We saw people rising to conquer new accomplishments right and left. I don't think a train could have stopped the success of this crew at that point.

A distinct turn signal of progress in the organization appeared when another department in the organization reached out to our department to help solve a problem. This came after several years of staying the course. A large contract had landed in our lap requiring yet more space. As word got out about the contract, a wonderful thing happened. The head of one of the other departments volunteered a collaborative remodeling of an entire wing that would house the new effort. I did not even have to ask. This was an emotional and beautiful example of people staying the course and learning to work together. The man leading the department had a wonderful attitude and was gracious in his proposal to work together. This visible act of volunteering a solution resulted in a beautifully remodeled wing, proved to be a turning point in the organization, and began building a more cohesive unity that had long been needed. It was a meaningful gesture of cooperation. Now the other pillar to complete the bridge had emerged to meet us.

> *We were on a mission, and any mission worth pursuing will be worth fighting for.*

As I reflect back on the leadership that was bred and fed, I believe that a few lessons have emerged with regard to Love, Celebration, and Excellence:

1. Love is at the top of the list. Loving people individually, seeing each one in their unique gifting and talent. Engaging them personally and inviting their contributions became a way of life. Everyone took a turn at leading meetings. People brought ideas without fear of looking dumb because our culture said there were no dumb ideas. We created room for people to grow and thrive in their respective power alleys.

2. Celebration was a type of glue for the group. It held us together especially during stressful

times. I recall one intense project where I had 40-60 writers and instructional designers working like crazy to design and launch a technical curriculum. Because of the size of the group and the nature of the work, we needed to create a cohesive atmosphere for the project to gel. I scheduled a cookout, delegated the decorations for a large picnic, had one of our team members bring her band, and we held a *jamboree**. The laughter, conversations, and beautiful music filling the air produced a congenial energy and cohesive spirit we needed to complete the job well.

3. Excellence in execution was the third success pillar. Keep the bar high and surpass it. That was my standard for excellence and nothing less was good enough. That means we established clear expectations for every contract or partnership we had, and then we met the milestones, and then some. Our reputation spoke for itself in the community and attracted those looking for stellar performance.

Did we mess up? Yes, and when we did I was the first one to deliver the news to the client along with our team's solution. It is so easy to react quickly or jump to the defensive and leave the root problem unaddressed. That means it will be coming back around. I also took the heat for my team. If they had an upset customer, they knew I was on call 24/7 to untangle, demystify, and put a situation on a positive path. I love doing that.

In the journey of this true story I have unfolded for you, we encountered many obstacles. There were many uphill battles to fight. We were on a mission, and any mission worth pursuing will be worth fighting for. We had our sites set on a goal and we went for it. We did it anyway.

What is your uphill battle? Where have you set your sights?
How will you do the thing you signed up for…anyway?

Even if it is hard… Even if you are criticized… Even if you get hurt?

Is your vision so clear and your commitment so firm that when you do enter the river of change you will know it is worth navigating the white water rapids?

What have you signed up for?

What are your rapids?

How do you show love for people in your workplace?

How do you celebrate accomplishments?

How do you model excellence in execution?

Notes for Action:

What is it that you will do,
ANYWAY?

CHAPTER NINE

What Matters Most

Knowing The God behind all your Whys

Journeys of life and business all lead to one thing – the opportunity to get to know the God behind all of your "Whys." Things come together when you realize what your ultimate quest is unto. This in no way minimizes your goals and dreams and vision; it gives them meaning beyond what you ever guessed possible. Getting to know your God catapults you into new realms of vision and understanding that make your former vision seem small. But we all have to start somewhere. We all have hoped to be part of something grander, more magnificent than we dared to dream. We have a secret desire to be great and to be a part of something greater. The battle over your secret destiny lies at the core of all of your life issues, problems, and desires. Now, *we're talkin' turkey*!*

> *The battle over your secret destiny lies at the core of all of your ...desires.*

When You Know That You Know

This is the gut factor...

Never ignore that "knowing in your gut." We all have it. I am referring to the "behind the scenes" information, which at times seems illogical. It can save your life or your business, if you pay attention.

When a concert artist allows you backstage, you see the real deal. You see the artist with his crew, his band, and his entourage. When a bellman in Las Vegas told me about the famous artists he had ushered into performances and limos, he said, "You'd be surprised what goes on behind closed doors."

The western world is extremely analytical and we pride ourselves on our ability to gather data, make projections, and predict the future. But the truth is, most of the time, the weatherman is wrong. Why is that? There are some things that require divine knowledge or insight. This insight goes beyond the facts and figures we normally rely on. We must learn to listen to His voice. Sometimes it is loud, but most of the time I have found it is a still small voice.

Lots of people brush aside these inclinations as their imagination or their own thoughts. I find when a person has put their life in God's hands through salvation in Jesus, the inside track of information makes all the difference in how we live, make decisions, and set priorities; it impacts the way we live our whole lives. We have a secret informant called the Holy Spirit.

What track are you on?

So what or who do you listen to? Who has the credibility to advise you and give you instruction on how to live your life and do your business?

Is it Oprah? Is it Dr. Phil? While these folks have a variety of ideas, I am not looking to put my life in the hands of another mortal human being. Nope, the stakes are too high. So I am looking up, looking to God for insight and revelation that will give me the insider secrets it takes to build the legacy I have in my heart.

So how do you get on the Inside Track?

You need to make a basic but important decision. It is the biggest decision you will ever make. Are you going to go with God? If your decision is to go with the God of the universe you could be prevented by one thing. You have no business talking to God because of sin. We all have it. And there is only one way past that obstacle: Jesus. He is the Way to God. He is the Truth personified. He is the essence of Life itself. Let me unpack that just a tiny bit. There is no other way to get to God, no other access point. He is your "free key" to unlock a door barred by sin— your only entry way to the God you desire. That is why you have to give up the guilt. You might think me narrow minded, but it would be narrow minded not to tell you the truth on this subject. Without this, nothing else in this book will get you far at all. So I'll ask you to stop right here, and ask God to help you hear this. Ask God to show you the heart of the matter. Ask Him to enter your life, because of what Jesus did, taking on your guilt. Now, here's the incredible news: God listens to this prayer every time, and answers.

God and Jesus travel with a third companion. When you ask Jesus to forgive you, God comes into your life and the Holy Spirit is now your teacher who has the inside track. Please don't think you can do this thing just to get the inside track. It does not work that way. It has got to be a real invitation. Simple is fine, but it has to be authentic. He loves you and wants you to engage with Him. Humbling, isn't it?

Letter to God:

In this space, write your own conversation with God based on what you have read in this chapter.

The God Behind Your Why

Come to know your God in the high times and low times. He is the same God in both seasons. Most people have heard the story of Job and how he had amassed a great fortune and a large family. He was the epitome of success... then it all fell apart. And when it did, everyone had an idea to offer. His friends figured that surely he was suffering because of secret sins in his life causing his world to crash down around him. They analyzed Job's situation always bringing the blame back to him. Obviously Job's inner circle of friends did not come through in the clutch. Job told his friends he had nothing to hide, but they were not convinced. Just because you love your friends and they love you does not mean their advice is right one hundred percent of the time. Perhaps Job needed a different inner circle. These people need to stand by you when the chips are down. Although it would be ideal, that does not always happen. Job's wife, whom you would think would be by his side even when everyone else was not, surprised him with her advice to just throw in the towel. "Curse God and Die," she said.

At the end of the journey, when we go to meet with God, we won't have our inner circle and family rallied around us to do business with God. Job's lonely journey of suffering brings home what I believe is the essence of why we are on this life-journey. Relax, it's not to suffer and have our lives fall apart! But it is to land where Job did at the end of his suffering. The *Why* is precisely that we would know God. Sadly we don't always get around to getting better acquainted with God, especially when we have a lot of props holding us up. In Job's example when his fortune was lost, his health crumbled, the family died, and the blessing of friends had dried up, he got to the main thing, the thing that matters most.

> *God's words meant more ....than his "necessary food."*

In his hard times, Job asked God the hard questions. He fell into despair, but in that dark season he came to terms with who God was to him. Job emerged out of the destruction as a man of hope. Job took the time to keep talking to God even when he did not get the answers he desired. Over the span of a long conversation with God we see Job turning from his questions into marveling, even raving about God's creation. Job even writes at one point that God's words meant more to him than his "necessary food." Job finally got to the essence of it all. He discovered what matters most.

Job also realized that hearing from God was what sustained him, even beyond food. He began to get to know His God.

I personally remember a time in our lives when Rick could not find a job to save his life. He valiantly searched for opportunities; he worked many jobs that seemed to hold no future. We could not figure out where we had gone wrong. Why would God not lead him into a good job? We were two fairly intelligent people, with good educations; we had not done anything so terribly wrong as to end up on the course of unemployment. Many people in today's economy are extremely talented and well educated but have found themselves without work.

We read Job's story during that time of our lives and reached the conclusion that God was after much more in our lives than just answering a prayer about a job. He wanted us. After we came to realize what the battle was about, many other things fell into place.

Job recognized who He was talking to: the God of the universe. He proclaimed God's majesty. Job realized God did not owe him the answers he was demanding. After this major breaking point, Job ended up with a greater fortune, a larger family, and more of everything than he'd ever had before. He had found his *Why Forward.*

Job died old and full of days. I want to die old and full of days, not wasted days, ill-spent days, or a trivialized life. To die full of days is not just a matter of age— it is a matter of wisdom. To know God, to gain insight, is to know wisdom, and we just touch the fringes of God's glory and majesty at that.

After Job's great loss he got a new view of God.

Job recounted:

> "I have heard of you with the hearing of the ear;
>
> But now my eye sees you." Job 42:5

You could write a novel about what happened between these two phrases in Job's life. Actually the novel already exists in the book of Job. But you have your own story to think about. Hearing is one thing; seeing is quite another.

A Cab Ride with Destiny

> *"I have heard of you with the hearing of the ear,*
> *But now my eye sees you."* Job 42:5

I had a very insightful discussion with a doctor, who specialized in burn treatment, 40 years after my fire experience. I was in Chicago for a professional meeting and shared a cab from the airport with a gentleman headed to the same hotel where I was staying. As we made small talk in the cab, he explained that he was attending a medical convention and that he was a burn doctor. I had always wanted to share my story with a burn doctor and this was my day. I told him my story, and I even rolled up my pant legs to show him my legs in the cab. The interest and amazement on his face was evident when I told him that my 3rd degree burns healed without skin grafts. He went on to ask me about what type of treatment I had. I relayed to him the only significant thing I could remember about treatment which was the hot 100 degree whirlpool baths I was given two times a day. I was told it would fight infection and remove dead skin. It was painful and part of the daily routine. He was silent for a moment, and looked away.

Finally, he said, "We don't do that any more. The hot whirlpool treatment was found to spread infection and a significant percentage of people who received that treatment died from septic shock."

I was on a cab ride with destiny. A wave of chills came over me as I sat in that cab in the Windy City realizing that God had preserved me in ways I had never known before this day.. He had shown up big time and was fighting for me all along in ways I never dreamed of. We may never know just how many times we have been spared death.

Psalm 68:20 says, "God is to us a God of deliverances; And to GOD the Lord belong escapes from death."

If I had turned away from God back at that tragic time in my life, I shudder to think of all the time I would have wasted being mad at God. My life would have been very different.

What has occurred in your life after hearing *about* God... that makes you aware you are beginning to see Him *for yourself?*

Do you desire to envision God? Do you want to recognize Him around you, to hear His still small voice, even His thunderous proclamation of love to the earth?

I challenge you to journal and expressly begin to document all the ways you hear and see God over the next 90 days.

I did this once and it was such an exciting experience to open my eyes to how God was working and speaking all around me.

Watch for: simple impressions, profound realizations, encouraging words, and affirming events that show God is leading you or speaking to you—just pay attention. The Holy Spirit will show you the way.

We need to learn to look and listen for God. Just expect God to show up.

Get a separate journal and start capturing your impressions from God today.

Pass It On

It is amazing to see the effect that the lives of those around us have on us. The ones who have gone before us have laid foundations for us to build upon. And it is humbling to look at those who we hope to influence on their journey forward.

I tell people that we should always be learning, and we should always be teaching. Actually, we are all teaching *something*, but we may not be giving much thought to the impact our lives have on others. Our very lives teach something, good or bad with every interaction we have. I received an email just yesterday from an individual in reply to one of my coaching messages that bears this out saying, "You have coached me by your very life. I have watched you ..."

So who is watching you?

There is no neutral territory. Our life lessons are either building others up, giving others something to build on, or they are negative lessons that hold them back in some way.

There is a vast audience waiting to be taught.

I challenge you to take up this responsibility and look around for someone you can teach something good about how to live a better life. It shouldn't be hard to find a person you can begin to encourage. It can be formal or informal. We are better together than we are alone if we link up with people who share our common values and vision.

I've noticed over the years that Rick continually has a trail of young men gathered around him. He attracts those who want to be around a godly man, a good example.

It can be a young boy across the street intrigued at a hunting blind Rick is building, or may be young men wanting to learn archery skills. Just last week a young man voiced his desire to learn from Rick. He said, "The young men I know need more of Rick Fields." What you exhibit in your life will attract those who need or want what you have to offer.

For several years Rick had the opportunity to affect students in a prison population where he taught life skills in the Texas prisons. For many of these men, Rick was the first exposure they had ever had to a positive male role model. We have a stack of letters these men have written to him thanking him for the difference he made in their lives by just showing up every day, teaching in kindness, seeing them as individuals, and living in their view. He taught them by example, word, and deed.

We have found organic life mentoring is most effective when building up young adults. They spend time with us, they learn about marriage, what it is to be unified despite being so vastly different as Rick and I are. They discover how to get past life obstacles to a smooth plain where they can build their lives.

Knowledge is built on a progression of stages. Although the journey from head-knowledge to heart-realization can be a long trip its progress can be speeded by experience and observation up close and personal. Adults learn best from experience.

Many young adults have not had positive role models to learn from. They have had absent fathers, wayward mothers, or perhaps parents busy with just surviving themselves. In these situations, there is unlearning to do before the new paradigms of successful life skills can be integrated in their lives. Inner healing is sometimes what is needed to address deep hurts, counseling can be a good thing, but eventually the best therapy is walking alongside someone who possesses the character and qualities you desire for yourself. I suggest you look for someone who carries a way of life that you want to catch. People are hungry to meet someone in life who is authentic; they are tired of the stale cookie cutter approach, the carbon copy of what everyone else is doing or saying. Get in relationship with individuals up close and personal who are not afraid to be unique, individuals who are real.

Some have commented to me about my particular "signature style," after they work with me or have been in my home. My office furniture and my home have a distinct presence that is tangible. I have a certain style in my mannerisms, clothing, and speaking, and it's just me. My taste consists of wood desks, leather chairs, textured upholstery, leopard chairs, old books, different things I coordinate to produce a creative atmosphere. I don't think about it; it is just what I naturally do. I just like to do things up right. But my décor, my clothes, and the way I carry myself all sum up characteristics of my life that describe my unique signature style.

Rick on the other hand usually wears some type of camouflage, is a man's man, and loves the outdoors. We are clear on who we are, and we are clear on the fact that we belong together. Much of our strength in our relationship comes from our individual identities, both masculine and feminine, brought together in our marriage.

We often attract young men and women who want to know how to walk out their individual identities, by flowing in business, working in ministry, enjoying outdoor life, building a good marriage, nurturing good relationships, and living life to the fullest. We love the interaction, and it keeps us young.

Lessons that we learn from life are founded on wisdom and learned through experience. It is always a privilege to "give it forward." I also believe it is our responsibility to teach those around us.

Who do you attract? What do these individuals need to learn? The community experience alone is worth getting a group together for a few weeks to discuss life lessons and application. In this chapter, I have provided a guide for each of the 10 chapters (including this one) that you can immediately use with a group of people who want to get more out of life.

The guide contains discussion material and a few ideas on how to apply the lessons. I would encourage you to start a discussion in your business, organization, or community and reach out to share what you have to offer. Put your own creative slant on it, but the main thing is to begin giving forward.

We are so proud of the young people we have around us who have made the effort to grow and learn. (You know who you are.) You have responded to coaching and mentoring with teachable hearts. We are still learning ourselves; we never arrive and the day we think we do is cause for another life lesson. Being vulnerable, sharing your hard lessons, living out your *Why Forward,* running with an inner circle or home team is a fabulous way to get more out of life and bring out the leadership within you. The contagious joy of living your life authentically takes the pressure off to perform. You can simply be yourself. You laugh a lot more and you enjoy life more from day to day.

Building your legacy is something you do one day at a time. I challenge you to capture and add your own lessons to the ones I have written about here, build up the people you can find, and share what you have to offer.

And by all means,

Please pass it on.

*Bonus Guide for
Discussion and
Application*

128

DISCUSSION GUIDE

A few ideas on how to prepare...

Forming a Group

Consider how you can pass on these lessons to help others find their *why* and their way forward. Think of those who can learn along with you and invite them to join you on the journey.

You may find these people in your neighborhood, at work, in church, or simply by gathering a group of friends who desire more out of life.

How to Get Started:

Plan to coordinate a 10-session study. The ideas here will give you everything you need to get started.

Decide on a facilitator:_____

Choose your location: _____

Schedule your start date: _____

Make a List of those you will invite:

Order Your Resources:

1. Find Your Why Forward DVD set
2. Find Your Why Forward Books for each person
3. Find your Why Forward Workbooks for each person

Conducting the Sessions:

First Session: Welcome guests and pass out books and workbooks.

Show the Welcome Video and Lesson One Video.

Each video has a corresponding Video Keys guide sheet to be filled out as individuals listen to the video teaching. The Video Keys are located in the Find Your Why Forward Workbook at the beginning of each chapter.

Homework: Participants will read Chapter One and fill out the workbook with their thoughts prior to the next class. The workbook provides ample space for writing out answers to the questions in the book.

Second and remaining Sessions:

Group Discussion: The first 30 minutes - encourage the group to discuss the main highlights of their homework from the last session. Also, see the Discussion Guide in your book for specific exercises and questions for each chapter to use during this time.

Video Lesson: The next 30 minutes - watch the video for the next chapter.

Homework: is to read the next chapter and write responses in the workbook.

How to Use the Discussion Guide:

The Discussion Guide is designed to stimulate interaction and apply practical ways to integrate lessons into the lives of the individuals. Some of the chapters might take two sessions if you want to go more in-depth on a particular subject. Or, if you need to speed things up you can divide into small groups and split up the discussion questions.

Remember that these ideas are merely to get you started. Be creative and use this as a springboard to design a productive experience, adjusting it to fit your style and the needs and interests of the group.

On the following pages you will find points for Discussion and Application for each chapter:

1. You Are Not Your Struggle
2. Burned But Blessed
3. Finding Your *Why Forward*
4. Get a Larger Vision
5. No One Succeeds Alone
6. Life At Work
7. Money
8. Do It Anyway
9. What Matters Most
10. Take the Next Step

Whether the study is done by an individual, or a group, the more time spent in personal application of the principles and lessons, the more growth will be experienced. So resist the temptation to read for the stories. Instead, read with these question in mind,

"How can I apply this story or lesson in my own life? What can I learn? What can I do differently? How can I grow?"

Chapter 1

You Are Not Your Struggle - Discussion:

a) The sooner you can separate your identity from the pain of your struggle, the sooner you can build a healthy identity in God. Of course your pain shapes you and teaches you, but it is not your entire personality, is it? What is your failure? What has been your hardship? What is your condition? Had we taken the blow of Wal-Mart coming to town and decreasing our business at The Field House personally, we would still be sad and mad today. Things happen. Life goes on. This may sound cold, but we have to get over ourselves without losing ourselves. Everything that happens in your life is not a personal accusation against your identity. The devil would love for you to process it that way and that is a really mean trick.

b) The devil's job is to basically keep you from believing the Bible and loving God and accepting Jesus. The best way he can accomplish that is to keep you tripped up over something you believe has been done to you so that you take on a life identity of being wounded or hurt and suffering.

c) "Rejection" is the name of his game. I am amazed at the huge insight on this very subject found in the Bible in Revelation 12:10 where we see the devil's job description is to be an accuser. He accuses you of anything that will get your attention and has the potential to get you down. It can be what others think of you, how you failed when you tried to act on what you thought God told you, any personal failure, bitterness, or pain. He is relentless at accusing you day and night

d) Now is there an answer to all this chaos? Yes, in the very next verse we find this great and hopeful solution.
"And they overcame him by the blood of the Lamb and by the word of their testimony..." Rev 12:11. Jesus has already done His part. His blood was shed on the cross. Now comes your part—overcoming with the word of your testimony. That means there is power in what you speak out of your mouth; that is the word of your testimony.

You can agree with your accuser about a problem or accusation. The accusation route shuts you down.

Or

You can choose to agree with your destiny in God and go forward overcoming the accusations. This route allows you to stay open and approachable in life.

e) Another verse says you can choose life or choose death. Well I am thinking life would be the better choice here, would you agree? With every word, deed, action, and belief of your heart you can choose life over death.

So agreeing in this context means more than just voicing a few positive words. It means speaking the life-giving words and lining your life up accordingly.

Your actions should agree with your words. Walk your talk.

You Are Not Your Struggle - Application:

You will need two or three index cards for this application.

1. Write on one side of each index card an accusation you struggle with. It can be a feeling of being looked down on, it may be what you feel others might think of you, or something you think about yourself because of the past.

2. Find a verse in your Bible that gives you God's view of your situation. Turn the card over and write your verse. Then write out a new statement about your situation that agrees with God's view.

3. Share one of your ideas if you are comfortable doing so with another person in the group and pray for each other. Keep your cards visible all week, and any time the accusing thought comes to mind, get out your cards and read your verse and statement aloud.

Chapter 2

Burned but Blessed - Discussion:

The finest china must endure the hottest fire. That is not very comforting if you plan on becoming fine china, but it does explain some things.

a) In a fire, the reflection of the potter's face can be seen when the china is "done." Whose face is evident in your life as the result of your time in the fire?

b) Is it the face of pain and bitterness or resentment for being held back? Is it joy at having come through the fire with wisdom and a reflection more like God's than when you went in?

c) Well, I am talking brave here, but this is a continual journey. It is not a one-time fix. You can waste your time in the fire if you don't decide to go for the reflection that is indicative of growth.

d) Business fires can be as devastating as bankruptcy, failure, or lack of success. In today's economy many are struggling with the fire of unemployment only to find themselves highly credentialed with nothing to do and no paycheck.

e) The one who emerges from the fire blessed is able to see the next opportunity, the way forward, with a hint of the Master Potter's character and wisdom etched in your countenance. This is no small work. It is the hardest work you will ever do. So coming out of the fire refined and blessed is the goal.

f) My fire taught me several things that have helped me in business. The first and most important lesson was that God heard a young person's prayer, and why would He not hear me now? He always has. The second lesson was to learn to stand. I spent time in physical therapy on a special table being tilted upright a little more each day until my legs could once again bear my weight. My legs were wrapped tightly in ace bandages because the skin was tissue paper-thin and would break at the slightest brush or added pressure. Eventually though I could stand.

g) Then there was learning to walk. I went through a very awkward experience to be 14 years of age and bumbling around with no sense of balance. I had railings to hang onto at first to steady me. Eventually, a walker replaced the railings, then free form— whee! Sometimes I made it without falling and sometimes I toppled to the side to be held up by a physical therapist standing ready to help.

h) In business when you are burned, you first survive the fire. You talk to God a lot. You come to a place when you have to decide to venture out again risking falling again or being embarrassed if you stumble.

i) There are no guarantees you won't fall or stumble. You can just sit in a wheel chair, figuratively speaking, for the rest of your life and not try again. That would be the sensible thing to do. After all, you have an excuse now for being in the wheel chair, right? People will understand.

j) Now, do you want to set aside your destiny to never get up again? I am just asking because you can do this either way. Find out how many times President Lincoln failed. Find out how many times George Washington Carver tried experiments that failed.

Burned but Blessed Application:

In thinking over your own experiences of getting burned, answer these questions:

1. In what way do you have to learn to walk again in your life?

2. Define for yourself any guardrails you might need to put in place: safety nets or supports to help you while you are learning to walk again. What would that look like?

3. Enlist a friend to be your spotter or person to steady your walk.

4. Find a Buddy to team up with:

    a. Who will you ask to be your buddy?

    b. When are you meeting?

    c. Where are you meeting?

    d. What's your plan?

Chapter 3

Finding Your Why Forward – Discussion:

1. If you are married, let's talk about that a minute. How is it going? Oh, I see, not what you thought. Hmmmm. Ok, well here's the thing. I love Rick more now than I did the day we married. We grew into this love by sticking it out. It hasn't always been easy; we have weathered unemployment, struggling to find our way, making sense of things that were different that we imagined. But oh, to stay and to grow old with someone, loving them, being loved and known. This is a beautiful thing. So many young people can't believe we've been married for 38 years and still love and like each other. That makes me sad because people need to see you married people thriving in relationship. Work it out. Quitting is too easy these days. Love is a commitment and there is a way for you to find going forward. For all of us, there's a principle in this lesson about love that is much larger than marriage, and we all need to get this.

2. Love is a Man named Jesus. With Him here is no rejection or pain, no problem you have that He does not understand. And what's more, He has made a way for you to know Him, to get to know God so you can have a full life. God is love. We've trivialized the word love because we say that we "love" pizza, iPhones, and cruises, but God is the true definition of Love. He loves you so much. You need to know that and get in touch with the reality of this great love God has for you personally.

3. His love encompasses your life, your family, your work, your friends, —the whole spectrum of your life. Knowing God's love changes everything else. When you are sure He loves you, a lot of other stuff loses the power it once held over you.

4. You are not your job or your business. You are an individual uniquely created and loved by God. Read Psalm 139

5. We've all messed up. Sometimes it is a big mess sometimes it is a bunch of little problems, but either way, relief is available to those who simply ask forgiveness. We had a worker from our Field House store who returned to Rick several years later and asked forgiveness for stealing a tennis outfit from us. We had never suspected a thing. He had graduated from college, moved away and gotten a job. He came back through town and came in to see Rick at the store one afternoon. In their conversation he told Rick what he had done and said he just could not sweep it under the rug any longer. He asked Rick to forgive him and insisted on paying for the stolen items. Rick was very impressed by their interaction and blessed the young man as he went on his way. The former employee had unloaded his guilt and left that day with a much lighter heart. The weight of guilt is weight that will affect you greatly and there's no need to carry guilt. Jesus paid a price for all the things imaginable that we've done wrong or will do wrong.

He forgives.

6. You may wonder about something you have done to a person who is no longer living or that you cannot communicate with for some other reason. Simply write a letter sizing up the situation and asking God to forgive you. After you pray about it, rip it up.

Repentance brings times of refreshing.

7. You may need to forgive someone really important like God. So has God done anything wrong? No, in fact He was there even in the times you thought he was a no-show.

Give up the Guilt.

Finding Your Why Forward – Application:

Describe in a few sentences a time in your life when you thought God did not come through for you.

Now pray this simple prayer:

> God, please show me where you were during this time in my life?? Wait on Him to give you a sense of His presence.
>
> Record your impressions here:

When I heard the doctor in the cab in Chicago tell me how the treatment I was subjected to day-in and day-out had killed so many people, I thought, Oh God, you WERE with me even in those times when I had no idea how much danger I was in.

What should have killed me, could not wipe me out because God was there, protecting me in the shadows.

I've had many people have life changing experiences by praying this simple prayer. We spend so much of our lives pained over what might have been, what could have happened, IF ONLY...

"IF ONLY's" can take you to the grave without ever having lived full-out. Don't miss today for worry over yesterday.

If you feel God let you down, it is ok to tell Him that. Ask Him to forgive you for holding Him at a distance.

Many times the hardest person to forgive is yourself. Work through this at all co No one is perfect; we have all blown it.

Let it go and Let Him guide you.

All that bitterness and sadness builds up a wall that makes it hard to hear God. Taking down this barrier opens up for you a new lease on life.

   a) Who do you need to ask to forgive you?

   b) Who do you need to forgive?

Chapter 4

Get a Larger Vision – Discussion/Application Combined:

1. Write out a vision statement using this template:

   I (name)_____ will (action)

   _____
   _____

   Using my talents of

   _____
   _____
   _____

   Evidence of my walking in this vision will be:

   1. Impact

      _____

   2. Influence

      _____

   3. Other evidence that will be a sign of your walking out your vision:

After everyone has written their vision statements, share them with the group. As a group, affirm each individual and pray for each person to walk out his vision in power.

Chapter 5

No One Succeeds Alone –
Discussion/Application Combined:

In the business arena you need to be in community with other people who are for you. It is cut throat out there, and it is not for sissies! Finding and developing relationships with your inner circle and rallying together to network and support each other gives each member a huge boost of confidence. I have a network of business buddies I meet with twice a month at a coffee shop. We have a simple little routine consisting of sharing what projects we are focusing on currently, praying for each other, and sharing wisdom over some good coffee. The next week we ask each other how it is going and we do the same thing again. Something so simple is hugely important in establishing a base of support. We all need to know people who believe in us, who "have our back," so to speak.

I go over my goals and vision with one of my trusted professional friends in a significant way every year. In fact we've created a pretty cool process we use to speak into each other's lives and plan the next season. We speak more often to touch base. This context and history is a solidifying force that propels me forward in uncertain times.

1. Who do you consider your inner circle?

2. Who do you need to reach out to and encourage in their goals and vision?

3. Do you have a mentor? Who are you learning from that is a trusted source of wisdom?

Chapter 6

Life at Work - Discussion/Application Combined:

1. What are your top 3-5 values?

2. How do you exhibit your values in these settings:

   home?

   work?

   community?

3. What is a work related problem you are facing?

   Find a scripture that speaks to this issue.

   Write a prayer about the problem.

   Develop an action plan based on your scripture.

Chapter 7

Money - Discussion/Application combined:

1. Do you have a budget?

2. Discuss types of budget plans and resources.

3. Develop a Dream Budget as described in this chapter.

4. Create a presentation you could give to promote your dream to a group in the community.

5. Make your presentation to your group at a scheduled time.

Chapter 8

Do It Anyway – Discussion:

1. When you decide to go for new territory in business by expanding your business, or starting a new business, just face the fact that you will have people in your life who don't like what you are doing.

2. Often they feel left out just because you are moving ahead. Your progress just happens to be the agent to surface their own fear and insecurity. If you are progressing, they think it makes them look bad. Often the people closest to you can't fully appreciate what you are doing. It is not really personal, but then it can feel personal.

3. Knowing that you will encounter resistance or at least many who doubt what you are doing, you need a success strategy in place.

4. My SPARK™ success strategy encompasses all of the principles I am teaching you here. Don't leave out any of these principles if you want a complete strategy for success.

5. Half of this battle is knowing that the dark side of success does exist and may knock on your door. Now, as to how you answer the door, that is your secret weapon. You will need to be sure you have your act together.

Do It Anyway – Application:

1. Review your strategy by talking about these components in your life. If you have not put these things in place, do it this week. You should have a plan for success that starts with these things as a framework:

   a. Share your Clear Vision Statement:
   b. Who are your Business Buddies?
   c. Who is your Inner Circle?

2. Prayer Strategy:
   a. What is your Business or Ministry objective?
   b. Do you have a Key verse? If not ask God for one this week.
   c. Write out your Prayer for success:
   d. What are the Specific Prayer times you and others are praying about your business?

3. The way you emerge from the dark side of success has a lot to do with your next level of advancement. This can be your stalemate or your launching pad. Pray for each other to emerge strong and ready to move forward when testing comes your way.

4. During the week, refer to the SPARK system in your book for ideas to enhance your leadership skills.

Chapter 9

What Matters Most – Discussion:

When You Know that You Know

1. Discernment, understanding, looking at timing—these are things you can develop and grow in over time. What I would recommend is that you take good notes always, pray about things seriously in your life and business, rely on good solid Business Buddies, and listen to the Holy Spirit. Walk things out with wisdom and with trusted advisors. Journal, pray, be teachable, and stay in a community of like-minded people going where you want to go.

2. Don't ignore your gut. You will regret it later.

3. Don't assume you know EVERYTHING there is to know.

4. A lot of this insider information is for you to just be aware of and pray for people or for situations. Exercise caution. Don't go preaching it on the street corner. Be smart, be an observer, be a note taker. It is *insider* information, remember? This is not to impress people with or to flaunt.

5. This is about gaining perspective and wisdom to understand times and seasons.

What Matters Most – Application:

1. Pretend that you are at the end of your life. You have had a life of success as you define it. You have touched people, earned money, blessed others, and done the things you believe you were born to do.

2. Describe what you would hope that looks like for you specifically:

3. The ultimate success of lasting value in my life will be how well I've gotten to know God. A verse that is a favorite of mine personally is found within Daniel 11:32b- 33a. "The people who know their God will have strength and take action (or do great exploits). Those who have insight will give understanding to many." This verse is in a chapter talking about some big time events yet to unfold, but it has application for the present as well. Now just for a moment, let's unpack this verse.

   a. Who is going to have strength?

   b. Who is going to take action?

   c. Who is going to do great exploits?

4. So what are you doing to know God?

5. Are you reading the Bible or going to a study? Are you doing an online study?

6. Some people leave things like knowing God to theologians, but this is for every man or woman.

Knowing God comes by not giving up when we don't understand or when life gets hard. It is a daily conversation. Just like I got to know my husband over years of communicating, working through the good things and bad things in life, I am getting to know God the same way.

The Holy Spirit is a helper, a teacher. So don't believe that you can't know God. This is the "big deal," and He gives supercharged insight and perspective to everything about your life. Jesus did most of His teaching and relating to people out and about in the marketplace. What were we thinking, leaving all that to Sunday school or to church classes? Out here in the business world is the most exciting opportunity to know God, have strength, and take action.

7. What great exploits are on your mind? What do you want to accomplish with your life?

8. What unfinished business do you have with God?

9. How can you join those two questions (7 and 8 above) and get to know God in your business?

Chapter 10

Take the Next Step

As you complete Chapter 10 with your group plan a special time of launching to celebrate each member in this last meeting. You may want to have a dinner or banquet setting where each member brings friends or family to share in this significant event.

Ask members of the group to share their ideas and plans, specifically have them bring their Journey Maps, from the Find Your why Forward Journal, to solidify how they will apply the lessons from this experience personally and how they will challenge others with what they have experienced. How will they raise the bar for themselves and others? What was the most important chapter in the book or big Aha moment for them?

Have time to give feedback to each member encouraging them to intentionally live out the individual authentic Why within each one with new courage and boldness.

Close with a time of blessing.

I celebrate your journey
of personal transformation
as you complete this final chapter.

Your relentless desire to
Find Your Why Forward
is beginning to pay off with:

Progress towards your Goals
Greater Confidence
Authenticity
Better Relationships.

Now it's time to Take the Next Step…

Take the Next Step

Congratulations on making it this far!

You've completed this leg of the journey. The principles you have learned and discussed are equipping you to live your life full out. By now you are thinking of people you can impact with what you have learned. This journey of passing it on becomes a way of life. You see beyond yourself and plug into something bigger than you. As you see the people you are helping grow and succeed, your joy increases. It's contagious. Your leadership is evident and growing, your life is full. You are learning to live a life that is full of days like Job did, one wise decision at a time. You are stepping into your greatness.

Who can you mentor?

Who are your "sons and daughters?"

How will you reach them?

Where is your Tribe or Community?

I am inviting you into a community or a group of people who will take a leap of faith every time they hit a wall. As you grow, you're going to see your *Why's* and *Why Not's* become your Way forward… your *Why Forward*.

You will see your vision become more clear, your leadership will rise up, your joy will burst out, you will be doing what you were made to do, in God's strength.

The people who have strength and take action are the ones who know God. These are the leaders who will accomplish great and noble things.

Are you in?

Let's go together.

Go to www.LindaFields.org and join your community.

Texas Talk Glossary

Upset the Apple Cart = Stir up negative emotions

Blue Sky—Anything goes or the sky is the limit

Hubbub—Big deal or an uproar

Jamboree—A noisy celebration, big party with lots of BBQ, and loud music

Pistol-packin' mama—A woman who has a gun and knows how to use it

Shakin' and bakin'—Get moving

Talking Turkey—Getting down to business; discuss a problem in a serious way with real intention to solve it

Whole Enchilada—Everything rolled up in one tortilla

ABOUT THE AUTHOR

Linda Fields, MBA, works with individuals, business owners and leaders to deepen vision, improve results, and launch destiny. She leads leaders, builds successful businesses and teams, positively impacts her local community, and serves organizations and individuals from around the globe. She lives with her husband of 37 years in the Kansas City area.

Linda mobilizes people in personal destiny and clarifies organizational vision through:

> *Retreat to Advance events*

> *Leadership Coaching*

> *Motivational Speaking and Training*

For more information including a special gift for readers, visit www.LindaFields.org